I0042547

The Scottish Social Worker's Practice Learning Handbook

This book provides a guide to social work education and continuing learning in Scotland. It promotes an effective learning ecosystem for the social work profession.

Split into three parts, specific issues facing Scottish social work learners and educators are outlined. Part One explores the context of social work education and continuing learning in Scotland, Part Two focuses on the learning journey across career stages and Part Three explores how effective learning environments are developed with attention to supporting relationships.

The content aligns with the Standards in Social Work Education, the Newly Qualified Social Worker Supported Year in Scotland and practice education qualifications to offer a comprehensive and invaluable volume that supports effective professional learning at all career stages.

Gillian Ferguson is Doctorate in Health and Social Care Programme Leader at the Open University. Her research interests are in professional, workplace and practice learning. She is a Senior Fellow of the Higher Education Academy, member of the British Association of Social Workers and Affiliate Member of the Chartered Institute of Personnel Development. Gillian is a registered social worker in Scotland who has previously worked across third sector and statutory settings. She has also worked in learning and development roles and was former lead for the Practice Learning Qualification delivered by the Tayforth Partnership. She remains an active practice educator in Tayside.

'This is a fantastic book focused on professional learning across the career aligned with Scottish standards, policies and resources. The author is well-versed in all aspects of professional and practice learning, remains active as a practice educator and is passionate about creating a flourishing learning environment for social workers.'

Kathryn Baker, *CEO Tayside Council on Alcohol*

'As a social work academic, I can see myself using this book in my work across programmes – it is relevant for social work academics, social work students, practice educators, link workers and learning advisers within practice settings. The approach to career-long learning and the Scottish context is a key strength.'

Dr Maggie Bruce, *Senior Lecturer in Social Work, University of Dundee*

'This book is relevant and timeous for Scotland, and its explicit focus on learning through practice is useful for learning and development teams to support how organisations respond. The author's recent research has already gained recognition and has been used to think differently about learning in social work.'

Billy Fisher, *Chair Social Work Scotland, Learning and Development Network*

'This book covers many current issues which are influencing social work practice learning and education today. The focus on practice learning in Scotland is particularly welcome. The author is well respected for her experience in direct practice, social work education, practice education and professional development.'

Avril McIvor, *Former Director of Practice Learning, Honorary Fellow in Social Work, University of Edinburgh*

The Scottish Social Worker's Practice Learning Handbook

Gillian Ferguson

Routledge
Taylor & Francis Group

LONDON AND NEW YORK

Designed cover image: Getty Images

First published 2026
by Routledge
4 Park Square, Milton Park, Abingdon, Oxon OX14 4RN

and by Routledge
605 Third Avenue, New York, NY 10158

Routledge is an imprint of the Taylor & Francis Group, an informa business

© 2026 Gillian Ferguson

The right of Gillian Ferguson to be identified as author of this work has been asserted in accordance with sections 77 and 78 of the Copyright, Designs and Patents Act 1988.

All rights reserved. No part of this book may be reprinted or reproduced or utilised in any form or by any electronic, mechanical, or other means, now known or hereafter invented, including photocopying and recording, or in any information storage or retrieval system, without permission in writing from the publishers.

For Product Safety Concerns and Information please contact our EU representative GPSR@taylorandfrancis.com. Taylor & Francis Verlag GmbH, Kaufingerstraße 24, 80331 München, Germany.

Trademark notice: Product or corporate names may be trademarks or registered trademarks, and are used only for identification and explanation without intent to infringe.

British Library Cataloguing-in-Publication Data
A catalogue record for this book is available from the British Library

ISBN: 978-1-041-16006-9 (hbk)
ISBN: 978-1-916925-93-9 (pbk)
ISBN: 978-1-041-05759-8 (ebk)

DOI: 10.4324/9781041057598

Typeset in Optima
by codeMantra

This book is dedicated to the wonderful social work practice learning community in Scotland.

Contents

Figures

Tables

Acknowledgements

Thanks to all my former comrades in the Tayforth partnership for inspiring me throughout my involvement in practice learning and trusting me to lead the practice learning qualification on our behalf. I hope I have done us justice. Special thanks to Daniel Piggins and Linda Grierson for having conversations with me and sharing their experience to help shape some ideas. Thanks also to the guru Brian Smith, formerly of the Scottish Social Services Council (SSSC), for his eternal wisdom on all things regulation, standards and his great company in many endeavours. Gratitude is also expressed to everyone who has encouraged me in the process of writing this book; it is sincerely appreciated. Any research participants cited within this book are anonymised.

Introduction

Fàilte

Welcome to *The Scottish Social Worker's Practice Learning Handbook*

This book is for social work students, social workers, practice educators, academics, strategic leaders and anyone else interested or involved in social work learning and education in the Scottish context. It was written in a conversational style, designed as a guide to social work education and continuing professional development in Scotland which highlights the importance of learning in practice. It promotes the concept of an effective learning ecosystem for the social work profession in which we can all play a part. This book outlines the specific issues facing Scottish social work learners and educators.

Social work is an extraordinary profession rarely understood by those who have not been immersed in it. Debates about the role and tasks of social work remain fraught with ambiguity. There is a deep-rooted public and political ambivalence about the profession. Within this context, defining the knowledge and skills that social workers require and facilitating their learning is incredibly complex. This book does not seek to teach all aspects of the social work curriculum, for which there are multiple other texts and resources; it intentionally focuses on learning in and through direct practice. It aims to be of value to social workers and those who support their learning across the whole of the professional career. The style and structure of each chapter integrate reflective and practical resources to promote critical thinking. You might choose to read through the chapters in sequence or select those most relevant to you, your current role and interests.

The impetus for writing this book stems from powerful accounts of the lived learning experiences of social workers, from leadership accounts in Scotland and from my different roles over time. Research into these lived experiences produced new ways to conceptualise social workers' learning that are firmly embedded in the book. I have always been interested in the transformative power of learning, working in community development, youth work and adult education before qualifying in social work. I am currently a lecturer in social work across the different United Kingdom nations but remain active in direct social work practice. I have worked extensively as a practice educator, as a local authority learning and development lead and as a programme lead for the partnership delivery of a Practice Learning qualification, and I also worked in the Scottish regulator. It is from these different perspectives that I have been immersed in social work education and learning. Everything that I have learned that underpins my practice, however, has its origin in learning as a volunteer support worker in the Scottish Rape Crisis Movement. This provided a foundation in understanding that there are many things we can only learn from people themselves about their lives and how they are best supported.

DOI: 10.4324/9781041057598-1

This book is also inspired by incredible colleagues in the practice learning community. Scotland has an incredible tradition of practice education from which wisdom, leadership and passion for ethical practice have been shared down generations. I have had the privilege to work with outstanding colleagues throughout my involvement in social work and hope that our shared passion and interests are represented throughout this book.

Part One outlines the context of social work education and continuing learning in Scotland and promotes the concept of an effective learning ecosystem for the profession. It explores some key milestones in social work, reminds us of important lessons from research and suggests that strong leadership and connections across the sector are essential for professional learning to flourish. The importance of learning in direct practice at all stages of the social work career is highlighted and illustrated by evidence from social workers' own accounts. The role of people who are working in human resources, workforce or organisational development roles is also positioned as pivotal in the responsibility for planning social workers' professional development.

Part Two develops an understanding of what learning as a social worker involves across career stages. This is designed to support social work students, qualified social workers and practice educators to maximise opportunities to learn in direct practice. Learning from the early stages of study right through the career involves a deeply personal journey. The chapters consider how social workers can develop the skills and knowledge required to do their extraordinary job. The chapters are aligned with the Standards for Social Work Education, standards for the Newly Qualified Social Worker Supported Year in Scotland, Scottish Practice Education Qualifications and Continuing Professional Learning requirements and promotes understanding of these.

Part Three explores the theory and practice of creating inclusive, effective environments for learning with the specific nature of social services contexts in mind. The discussion also considers the diversity of settings for practice learning in integrated, partnership contexts. Understanding the roles, tasks and functions of practice educators and workplace supervisors in assessing learners against standards and frameworks is fundamental to the learning landscape. Developing effective relationships to supervise, facilitate and assess the learning of individual students is discussed drawing on examples and expertise from the practice learning community in Scotland. Professional supervision is positioned as a key leadership space in which learning is promoted, inspired and supported across career stages. The chapters also centralise the importance of learning from the lived experience of people who use social work services.

The conclusion looks to the horizon of social work education and professional learning in Scotland. A guide to resources, places and spaces students, social workers, mentors, link workers, practice educators, human resource professionals and other colleagues have found useful for supporting learning is included at the end of the book.

Social work is perpetually reported to be at the cusp of transformation. Indeed, at the time of writing, many of us are watching the current strategic and operational landscape for social work in Scotland with bated breath. Whatever shape social work takes, the underpinning ethos of this book is that if we strengthen professional learning, we strengthen the social work profession itself. It is hoped that you enjoy reading about learning whatever your interest or role in social work in Scotland.

Written mostly on location in different bits of Scotland (and a tiny bit from the British Library in London).

Gillian Ferguson

A learning ecosystem for social work in Scotland

Part One

A learning ecosystem for social work in Scotland

Chapter 1

Social work education and continuing professional learning in Scotland

Introduction

This chapter outlines the context of social work education and continuing professional learning (CPL) recognising the specific nature of the landscape for learners and educators in Scotland. A summary of developments in social work education and arrangements for practice learning is briefly introduced. Critical issues raised in previous research about social work education and CPL are also explored. This chapter concludes by looking to the future landscape for learning in social work, proposing that important messages and our collective national expertise must not be forgotten.

Chapter aims

By the end of this chapter, you will be able to:

- understand the landscape of social work practice learning in Scotland;
- summarise critical messages from Scottish research;
- identify challenges and opportunities for future development.

The social work landscape in Scotland

Scotland has a rich tradition of creative approaches to developing social work practice, often led by local partnerships, passionate social workers and educators. The landscape has evolved over time and continues to do so since the Regulation of Care (Scotland) Act (2001) through sociopolitical shifts, changing expectations of practice and the position of social work as a profession. Suggested as continually in flux (Daniel, 2013), and perpetually at the crossroads (McCulloch and Taylor, 2018), social work remains difficult to articulate to those who have never been immersed in it. This book does not explore all these shifts in depth but points to some events and evidence that contextualise where we are in Scotland. For a fuller analysis of how things have shaped in Scotland since the Social Work (Scotland) Act 1968, see Cree and Smith (2018) or Daniel and Scott (2018). The trajectory of social work education in Scotland, its perpetual review and debate about the alignment of education with practice is well documented by McCulloch (2018). A contextual paper, in relation to the Introduction of a National Care Service (NCS) also provides a picture to help us understand the past to help explain the future (Scottish Government, 2022).

DOI: 10.4324/9781041057598-3

Social work practice in Scotland

Social work is notoriously hard to describe and articulate even within its own ranks. The broad and visionary global definition remains a common reference point which stresses the practice-based nature of the profession (IFSW, 2014). The reality of social workers' experiences can be quite different from the social justice and humanitarian rhetoric expressed by the global definition (Moriarty et al., 2015). Social work is often described in terms of the reserved statutory functions which define the legislative authority of the profession (Scottish Executive, 2006). Social work extends far beyond the realms of this, operating in diverse service settings in the third sector, local authority and integrated partnerships with rich opportunities to learn in each. That social work remains a generic qualification is an important point for Scotland (Daniel and Scott, 2018).

Multiple policy agendas continue to drive priorities and jostle for prominence in Scottish social work. Expectations of learning programmes are at the mercy of these demands. This book gets back to the heart of learning in and through practice, centralising how social workers learn with people they are working with. Irrespective of specific frameworks, agendas and shifting priorities, the essence of social work remains focused on a dynamic, relationship-based approach in which the worker must 'manage complexity, risk, and uncertainty in professional decision making' (SSSC, 2024a) while promoting human rights and social justice.

Key influencers in the Scottish landscape

Scottish local government is made up of 32 elected councils which are at the fore of social work services across the country. There are different configurations of how services are organised and delivered with these on the cusp of significant change (Scottish Government, 2022). There are many influential organisations and individuals who shape and/or control Scottish social work education and CPL shown in Figure 1.1.

The Scottish Social Services Council (SSSC), Confederation of Scottish Local Authorities (COSLA), Scottish Association of Social Work (SASW), Social Work Scotland (SWS), employers and universities are some of the key players. Social work education is provided by around nine universities, offering undergraduate and/or postgraduate qualifying approved programmes. Employers are fundamental to the delivery model for the Newly Qualified Social Worker (NQSW) Supported Year in Scotland (SSSC, 2024a). People who use social work services and social workers are highlighted as clear influencers but whether authentic involvement and co-production is actualised is important to reflect on. Debates about who owns the curriculum for social work is a further reflective point (Healy, 2019). Developments in Scotland have strived to be collaborative, however decisions about social workers' education and CPL are experienced in different ways across the sector.

SWS remains a powerful leadership body for the profession with an ambitious programme of work driven by members, committees and funded projects. SWS has hosted the Social Work Education Partnership (SWEP) over recent years which asserts that its aim is 'to futureproof social work education in Scotland by fostering national and regional partnerships' (SWS, 2024). SASW has an extensive activity representing the profession, provision of learning for social workers and professional coaching support. Social workers and others are rarely aware of the relationships and dynamics of the interplay between bodies that influence the profession. SWS and SASW are membership organisations, and

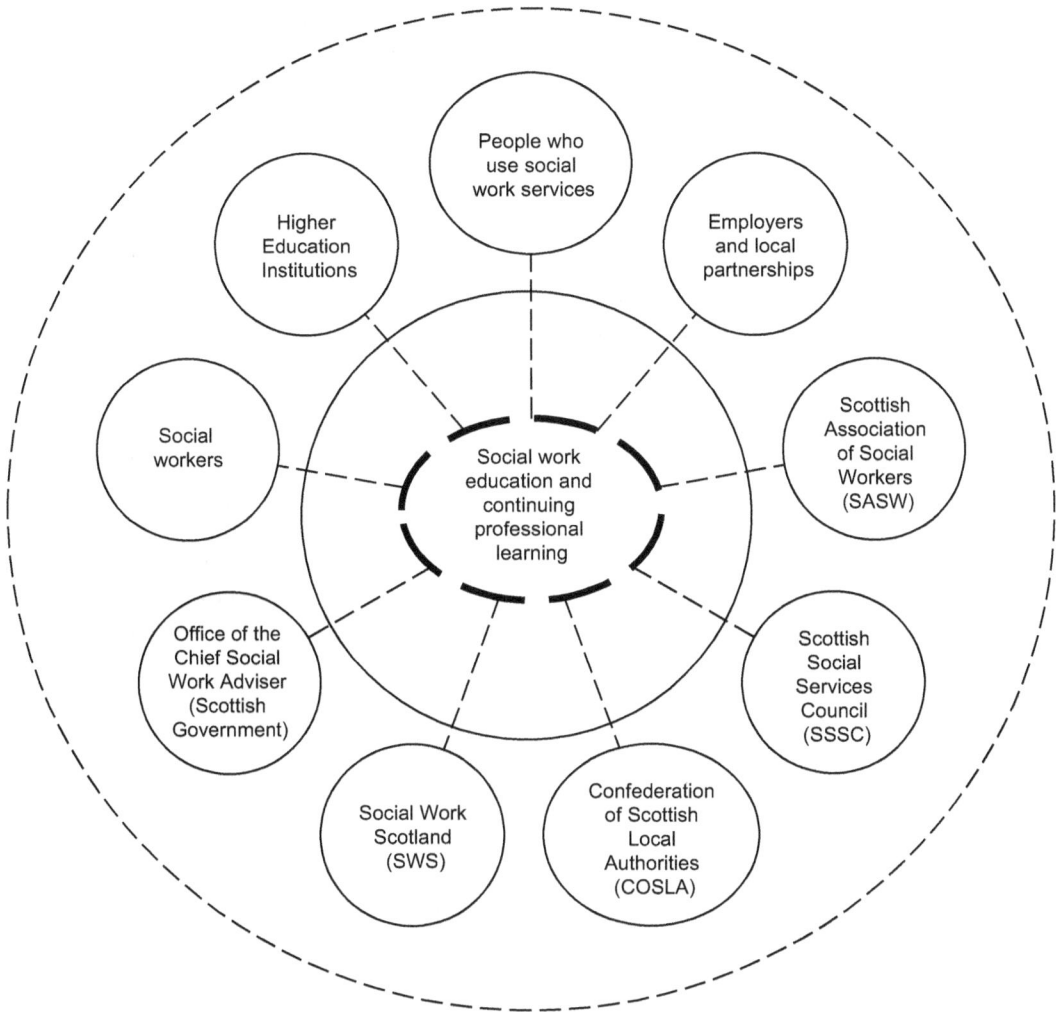

Figure 1.1 Influencers on social work education and CPL in Scotland.

although many social workers are not signed up members, most look to these organisations to hold and represent their interests in the political arena. Funding of different organisations and their overall relationship to the Scottish Government make for a complex landscape in which roles and relationships can seem intertwined. From 2025, a new Social Work Agency, an executive department of the Scottish Government, will emerge. A high-level Social Work Partnership will operate underneath this combining several of the key influencers and the landscape will continue to shift.

The regulation of social workers' learning

Within the United Kingdom (UK), each nation has a different framework and regulatory system for social work education and CPL, although there is alignment in the essence of these across nations. Social work education in Scotland is regulated by the SSSC under the Regulation of Care (Scotland) Act (2001). The remit and functions of the SSSC are not always widely understood in the sector.

For social work, SSSC responsibilities include:

- approval of qualifying programmes;
- approval of specialist awards such as the Mental Health Officer (MHO) Award and Practice Learning Qualifications (PLQs);
- all CPL requirements from the NQSW Supported Year and beyond;
- registration of social workers from the point of their entry to the register as students;
- return to practice requirements for social workers returning after a break.

The SSSC also regulates the wider social care and children and young people workforces in Scotland. Skills for Care and Development is the sector skills council, a partnership of four UK organisations who develop National Occupational Standards that underpin social work and social care qualifications. SSSC undertakes the functions of the Sector Skills Council in Scotland and is therefore central to all aspects of the skills and knowledge which are integrated into registerable qualifications for the workforce. There is a memorandum of understanding across the UK nations which allows students to register in the four nations (with the exception of some programmes from England which require compensatory measures in Scotland). Regulatory functions are unlikely to be at the fore of social workers' minds, but learning across the career is inextricably linked with the role of the SSSC and their rules, requirements and approach.

Reflective questions

- What do you know about the role of the SSSC?
- Who else shapes social work education and CPL in Scotland?
- Why is awareness of the regulatory context relevant for social workers?

You might not have thought much about these issues before. Many social workers have thought about their registration with the SSSC or the Codes of Practice (SSSC, 2024b) which inform all social service workers and employers. You might feel quite remote from the regulatory context. Awareness of the overall system that supports your learning as a social worker is important, and there are often opportunities to help shape future developments. Over 6,000 whole-time equivalent (WTE) practising social workers were recorded in Scotland in 2024, an increase of around 15% since 2019 (SSSC, 2024c). Official statistics show that this is the highest number since records began in the 1990s. This figure represents the number of social workers reported by local authorities, and a higher figure (over 11,000) was noted on the Social Worker register part (SSSC, 2024c). Over 2,000 social work students were also recorded on the respective register part at the same snapshot date.

How did we get here?

Looking into the rear-view mirror of social work education in Scotland can shine light on important messages for the current context. The Central Council for Education and

Training in Social Work (CCETSW), established in 1962 as the Council for Training in Social Work before changing name in 1970, approved and regulated awards across the UK. It ceased to exist on September 30, 2001, and many of its functions passed to the respective new care councils in each nation. Scotland's requirements shifted to a degree or equivalent postgraduate programme with the Framework for Social Work Education in Scotland (Scottish Executive, 2003) outlining Scottish Requirements for Social Work Training and the Standards in Social Work Education (SiSWE). This framework continued to position significant levels of supervised practice learning at the core of professional training. Requirements of preparation for practice and contrast between placements were also clear. A move to strengthen skills and knowledge in the protection of children quickly ensued with the development of Key Capabilities in Child Care and Protection (Scottish Executive, 2006) which sat alongside the SiSWE until their eventual review and published revision in 2019. A full further revision of the overall framework is due to be published in 2025–2026.

A treasure chest of research

There were multiple workstreams associated with the Review of Social Work Education in Scotland (RSWE) launched in 2013 which aimed to 'develop a new and different approach to professional learning in Scotland through a learning strategy that addresses qualifying and post-qualifying learning for the social service workforce in Scotland' (SSSC, 2015, p1). There is a treasure chest of evidence from research commissioned as part of the review across a broad spectrum of issues far beyond the SiSWE themselves. Each workstream involved collaboration with diverse key informants and partners across the country and review of arrangements in other nations. The original SiSWE ultimately did not need particularly substantial changes as much as the infrastructure around learning. The review led to some very clear recommendations (including arrangements for practice learning and post-qualifying learning, which remain unresolved over ten years later).

Evolution of the SiSWE

We have this extensive work from the RSWE led by teams of experts from universities, people using services and other partners. The cross-university collaboration reminds us that Scotland has a fantastic resource in the individual expertise and collective wisdom here. The SiSWE were revised and republished in 2019, strengthening some aspects. Many things looked the same, but the language, tone and emphasis were changed and some specific new standards were introduced notably: 'Develop opportunities for prevention and early intervention' (SSSC, 2019, Standard 2.1) and 'Support the wellbeing, safety and protection of vulnerable children and adults' (SSSC, 2019, Standard 3.3). The SiSWE remain a central component of the overall Framework for Social Work Education in Scotland which continues to evolve.

Reflective questions

- What do you think has changed in the SiSWE over time?
- In what ways are the SISWE important for the profession?
- Why are the SiSWE important for people who use social work services?

In the 2019 revision, clear responsibilities for protection of people across the lifespan became explicit, and the former Key Capabilities in Child Care and Protection were removed with the holistic revision of Standard 3. Use of self and emotional intelligence were also strengthened in the revision. Underpinning ethical principles were also introduced which are now also integrated in the model for the NQSW Supported Year launched in 2024. The ethical principles are closely aligned with the IFSW definition of social work, the SSSC Codes of Practice for Social Service Workers and Employers and the Health and Social Care Standards in Scotland (Care Inspectorate, 2017). At the heart of all this guidance are people's lives; therefore, the detail and focus are important. Specific knowledge requirements were also integrated, for example, issues around trauma and interpersonal violence, reflecting shifts in policy and practice priorities. It is always recommended to check for the most up-to-date, detailed versions of any standards as these continue to evolve.

Beyond the revised SiSWE

The evidence gathered as part of the RSWE is not widely remembered and has not always been harnessed to inform developments. Table 1.1 highlights the extensive collective expertise of colleagues across Scotland who carried out the research. The report on integrated learning (Kettle et al., 2016) is an incredible in-depth analysis of many challenges that remain current. The paper features a robust literature review and forms a detailed reference for considering how professional and practice learning can be supported in Scottish social work. The term 'shared professional learning' is proposed to describe 'learning in and between contexts that support development of professional competence and confidence as well as professional identity' (Kettle et al., 2016, p11). Responsibility should be shared across employers and educators, but endeavours remain fraught (McCulloch et al., 2024).

Although the SiSWE were revised, the overall Framework for Social Work Education with its component parts remained unfinished for many years. The teaching, learning and assessment requirements were eventually revised to clarify practice learning in terms of articulation of days, what counts as practice, contrast between placements and other

Table 1.1 A treasure trove of research from the review of social work education in Scotland

Overarching reports
Integrated Learning in Social Work: A review of approaches to integrated learning for social work education and practice   (Produced by a team from Glasgow Caledonian University and the University of Dundee)   Martin Kettle, Pearse McCusker, Louise Shanks, Richard Ingram, Trish McCulloch   *Is there a shared philosophy of learning across social work programmes and post-qualifying learning?*   (Produced by a team from the University of Edinburgh and the University of Dundee)   Trish McCulloch, Murray Simpson, Autumn Roesch-Marsh, Sheila Cooper   *What new skills will social workers of the future need?*   (Produced by a team from the University of Stirling)   Joanne Westwood, Kane Needham, Ian Watson

(Continued)

Table 1.1 (Continued)

Areas of enquiry on social work education

Revised Standards in Social Work Education and a benchmark Standard for Newly Qualified Social Workers
(Produced by a team from the University of Stirling)
Brigid Daniel, Sandra Eady, Sandra Engstrom, Jane McLenachan, Joanne Westwood, Nicola Yule, Brenda Gillies
Mapping of Standards in Social Work Education to the National Occupational Standards
Moira Dunworth, Jean Gordon
How can universities best select the right people for social work programmes?
(Produced by a team from the University of Edinburgh and the University of Dundee)
Viviene Cree, Gary Clapton, Mark Smith, Susan Levy, Richard Ingram, Fiona Morrison
To what extent should social work education have a stronger focus on community development and engagement?
(Produced by a team from the University of Strathclyde)
Graham McPheat, Ailsa Stewart, Gillian Macintyre, Sally Paul
Should there be a core curriculum and if so what should it include? (Produced by a team from Glasgow Caledonian University and the University of Dundee)
Pearse McCusker, Trish McCulloch
How can we maximise the impact of the collective experience of people who use social work services and their carers, in the design, development and delivery of social work programmes?
(Produced by a team from the University of the West of Scotland and the University of Strathclyde)
Debbie Innes, Jeremy Millar, Scottish Inter-University Service Users and Carers Network
How much of the qualifying programme should be undertaken with students from other professional groups, and how can these opportunities be maximised?
(Produced by a team from Robert Gordon University)
Janine Bolger, Mike Shepherd, Stephanie Creasy
What should practice learning look like?
(Produced by a team from the Open University and the University of Stirling)
Deirdre Fitzpatrick, Jane McLenachan, John Burns
What are the key characteristics of effective university/employer partnerships?
(Produced by a team from the Open University)
Jean Gordon, Roger Davis
What role can social work qualifying education play in developing social workers as leaders of the profession?
(Produced by a team from the University of Stirling)
Joanne Westwood, Catherine Pemble, Frances Patterson

Newly qualified social workers

Implementing a Probationary Year for Social Workers in Scotland: An option appraisal prepared for the Scottish Social Services Council
Brenda Gillies
Conclusions from research about the perceptions of Newly Qualified Social Workers (NQSWs) regarding preparedness and employer support
(Produced by a team from the University of the West of Scotland)
Scott Grant, Lynn Sheridan, Stephen Webb
Scottish First-line Managers' Views of Newly Qualified Social Workers' Preparedness for Practice – findings from an online Delphi study
(Produced by a team from the University of Strathclyde)
Vicki Welch, Jennifer Lerpiniere, Emma Young

Post-qualifying learning and development

Post Qualifying Learning Development Framework Report
Brenda Gillies

details. That social work practice must be assessed by a qualified practice educator who is a registered social worker is a significant strengthening of this revision in line with shifts in other nations. The RSWE also covered a wide spectrum of issues including recruitment processes, approaches to interprofessional learning, involvement of people who use social work services and expectations of the curriculum as shown in Table 1.1. The potential of qualifying education to position social workers as leaders of the profession was also a specific workstream (Westwood *et al.*, 2016) with leadership now embedded in the revised SiSWE and subsequent NQSW Core Learning Elements too (SSSC, 2024). A firm focus on options for a supported year in practice for NQSWs remained a high priority in the RSWE, albeit developments took until 2024 to be fully launched.

Partnerships and practice learning

It is no surprise that the perpetual issue of arrangements and partnerships for practice learning was a key focus in the RSWE. Scotland has wrestled with the availability of robust practice learning placements to meet the requirements of the profession, but many initiatives have supported this over time. The Scottish Practice Learning Project (SPLP) was a relatively well-resourced national initiative initially hosted by the SSSC before being amalgamated into it. One product of the SPLP was the development of quality standards and an audit tool for practice learning (SSSC, 2006) often still adapted for use in universities and organisations. During the life course of the SPLP, the voluntary nature of the audit tool may have hampered its embedded and sustained use. Scottish practice educators also had the benefit of a longstanding membership community in the form of the Scottish Organisation for Practice Teaching (ScOPT). ScOPT was at the fore of resources, information and activism for practice education across the nation until its sad closure in the early 2020s. Other initiatives such as the short-lived Practice Learning Scotland, a sector-led drive for developments in practice learning, chose not to progress in anticipation of the promise of SWEP.

Formal partnership arrangements have also supported learning and development for social workers across Scotland in previous decades; a few points are important to note. Four Scottish Social Services Learning Networks covering the whole of the country previously led wide-ranging activity. They directly coordinated and often delivered training, including PLQs, and they led the sector on emerging agendas such as leadership, mentoring and coaching in their heyday. These networks were characterised by authentic relationships between practitioners, services, academics and people who use social work services. Relationships with third sector and statutory services were also a key strength, and relevant sector reports on workforce planning or literature reviews were published by some networks. When funding for the networks ceased, relationships between partners remained strong in many areas with some continuing to work together on shared projects and even in the delivery of specialist awards. Learning Network West remained constituted as a formal network with local organisations and university providers until it was closed in November 2024. In Scotland, we also previously had other partnership arrangements such as consortia for the delivery and assessment of post-qualifying training (Coles, 2002). As new visions emerge, it is essential to be informed by the substantial evidence-base we have. Effective learning relationships are the focus of Chapter 9, and partnership approaches remain vital for the success of practice learning in any profession.

The position of practice in social workers' professional learning

Confidence in Practice Learning (SSSC, 2004) set the agenda for how the original degree qualifications in social work would be delivered with partnerships and resources key to success. SWEP was initiated following the RSWE, preceded by a 2018 meeting in which key questions were posed around what infrastructure would be needed to tackle the challenge of sufficient, consistent and quality practice learning. Practice learning remains central to the requirements for social work education, but arrangements for sustainable delivery posed in 2018 are yet unresolved. McCulloch *et al.* (2024) suggest that social work must confront its own failure to recognise and value the relationship between learning, research and practice and that local authority employers continue being unable to fill even basic student placement commitments.

The SSSC has always strongly promoted and valued informal and practice learning across social services. Building on earlier CCETSW frameworks, they focused on outcomes for people using services and that continuing professional development (changing their terminology to CPL at a much later time) 'encompasses a wide range of activities which contribute to lifelong learning' (SSSC, 2004, Section 3.3). Going further, they stated, 'it includes academic and practice development, and equally importantly, informal learning and learning and development in the workplace' (SSSC, 2004, Section 3.3). The position of practice is also unquestionable in the original Framework for Social Work Education and its subsequent revision. Confidence in Practice Learning stressed that it was 'everyone's business to support learning in practice' (SSSC, 2004, p9), the exact same call from Kettle *et al.* (2016).

Practice Learning Qualifications

The vision for PLQs that replaced the former Practice Teacher Award was broad and inclusive proposing a suite of qualifications at different academic levels (SIESWE, 2006). Current qualifications at Scottish Qualifications Framework (SCQF) Levels 10 and 11 are delivered through several universities and Scottish Credit and Qualification Authority (SQA) centres based in services. The original formal documentation about the PLQs remains the only current reference point for these qualifications. SSSC Rules and Requirements for Specialist Training for Social Service Workers, in which PLQs fall, are dated the same year. Opportunities to train as a practice educator have been subject to the rise and fall of different programmes across universities and local authority providers since the RSWE. Significant expertise sits with personnel who currently lead or have previously led delivery of PLQs and their impact on generations of social workers, practice educators and sector development cannot be underestimated.

Regulation of Practice Educators and their qualifying programmes differs across the UK, for example, in whether training courses are regulated as they are in Scotland or whether the person, their role or function is. This remains an arena in which we have started to see the regulation begin to shift in both England and Scotland, with emerging attention in Social Work England (SWE) and by the SSSC, in their review of the register (SSSC, 2024d).

Post-qualifying learning

There is currently no formal post-qualifying learning framework in Scottish social work although development of a new Advanced Practice Framework has been under development for some time. There are, however, clear requirements to maintain CPL for registration as a social worker and new standards set in 2024. There are also clear requirements for NQSW, and their employers, in the first year that they are registered (SSSC, 2024a). If you are a social worker, more discussion and ideas for your own learning and development are covered in the respective chapters in Part Two related to your career stage. If you are involved in or responsible for supporting social workers' learning, information for you is also woven throughout the book.

Looking to the future in Scotland

This chapter has scratched the surface of Scotland's rich history and context of evidence to inform professional learning. The implications of our past are important for what is yet to come. Leadership for learning, the focus of Chapter 3, involves all the key players at individual and organisational levels. Within a context which continues to shift, the importance of professional learning and its relationship to practice do not waver. Our future success relies on using evidence, research, collective leadership and practice wisdom across the sector.

Learning in practice

There is a constant challenge to navigate an external environment where there's national policy objectives … a framework for each and wee teams for each at Scottish Government, all those things are inherently not connected in terms of learning and development and improving practice, we could really do a kind of better cohesion at government level. How well does the rest of the system understand what social work does?

(Rory, Chief Social Work Officer, Research Participant, 2023)

Reflective questions

- What do you think are the most important lessons from the past?
- How do you think research and evidence can inform future development?
- In what way are you a key player in the Scottish landscape?

Summary points

- Scotland has a rich history of partnership and research in social work.
- Significant expertise about learning and education is held in the sector.
- Evidence from the treasure chest of research is often underutilised.
- Practice is positioned prominently in learning at all career stages.

Further reading

A quick read

The National Care Service contextual paper published by the Scottish Government to set the scene for emerging developments in social work provides a quick and comprehensive overview of the policy and practice landscape of Scottish Social Work (Scottish Government, 2022).

An interactive guide

The evolution of social work is charted, with helpful links to important Scottish milestones and further information, in the *Social Work Centenary Timeline* by the University of Edinburgh. This highlights key dates and recommendations about practice learning across the history of social work (Daniel and Scott, 2018).

A deeper dive

Integrated Learning in Social Work is an exceptional work from researchers at Glasgow Caledonian University and the University of Dundee. This is an essential reference for anyone exploring the future of social work education. Published under the Review of Social Work Education in Scotland, the report outlines the issues and debates that remain current (Kettle *et al.*, 2016).

Please also see the resources section in the Appendix.

References

Care Inspectorate (2017) *Health and social care standards* [online] https://www.gov.scot/publications/health-social-care-standards-support-life.

Coles, M (2002) *Post qualifying consortium for social work in Scotland* [online] https://mysssc.microsoftcrmportals.com/knowledgebase/article/KA-01850/en-us.

Cree, VE and Smith, M (Eds) (2018) *Social work in a changing Scotland*, First edition, Routledge, London.

Daniel, B (2013) 'Social work: A profession in flux', *Journal of Workplace Learning*, 25(6): 394–406, https://doi.org/10.1108/JWL-06-2012-0048.

Daniel, B and Scott, J (2018) *50th Anniversary: Social Work (Scotland) Act 1968* [online] https://socialworkscotland.org/projects/50th-anniversary-1968-social-work-scotland-act/.

Healy, K (2019) 'Regulating for quality social work education: Who owns the curriculum?', in Connolly, M, Williams, C and Coffey, D (eds) *Strategic leadership in social work education*, Springer, Cham, pp. 53–66.

IFSW (2014) *Global definition of social work* [online] www.ifsw.org/what-is-social-work/global-definition-of-social-work/.

Kettle, M, McCusker, P, Shanks, L, Ingram, R and McCulloch, T (2016) *Integrated learning in social work: A review of approaches to integrated learning for social work education and practice* [online] https://www.sssc.uk.com/knowledgebase/article/KA-01739/en-us.

McCulloch, T (2018) 'Education for the crossroads? A short history of social work education in Scotland', *Practice*, 30(4): 227–237, https://doi.org/10.1080/09503153.2018.1478956.

McCulloch, T and Taylor, S (2018) 'Becoming a social worker: Realising a shared approach to professional learning?', *British Journal of Social Work*, 48(8): 2272–2290, https://doi.org/10.1093/bjsw/bcx157.

McCulloch, T, Grant, S, Daly, M, Sen, R and Ferguson, G (2024) 'Embedding learning as a practice of value: Learning from the experiences of early career social workers in Scotland', *The British Journal of Social Work*, 54(7): 2977–2995, https://doi.org/10.1093/bjsw/bcae072.

Moriarty, J, Baginsky, M and Manthorpe, J (2015) *Literature review of roles and issues within the social work profession in England* [online] https://www.professionalstandards.org.uk/docs/default-source/publications/research-paper/literature-review-roles-and-issues-within-the-social-work-profession-in-england-2015.pdf.

Scottish Executive (2003) *Framework for social work education in Scotland* [online] https://www.gov.scot/publications/framework-social-work-education-scotland/pages/5/.

Scottish Executive (2006) *Key capabilities in child care and protection* [online] https://www.gov.scot/publications/key-capabilities-child-care-protection/.

Scottish Government (2022) *National care service: Social work contextual paper* [online] https://www.gov.scot/publications/national-care-service-social-work-scotland-contextual-paper/.

SIESWE (2006) *Practice learning qualifications 2006* [online] https://www.sssc.uk.com/about-us/publications/plq-framework-and-standards-2005-revised-november-2006/.

SSSC (2004) *Confidence in practice learning* [online] https://mysssc.microsoftcrmportals.com/knowledgebase/article/KA-01270/en-us.

SSSC (2006) *Scottish Practice Learning Project – Standards and audit for practice learning opportunities – A quality process* [online] https://mysssc.microsoftcrmportals.com/knowledgebase/article/KA-01650/en-us.

SSSC (2015) *Review of Social Work Education Statement on Progress*, SSSC [online] https://mysssc.microsoftcrmportals.com/knowledgebase/article/KA-01712/en-us.

SSSC (2019) *Standards in social work education,* Scottish Social Services Council, Dundee [online] https://learn.sssc.uk.com/siswe/siswe.html.

SSSC (2024a) *NQSW supported year overview and guidance 2024* [online] https://www.sssc.uk.com/about-us/publications/nqsw-supported-year-overview-and-guidance-2024/.

SSSC (2024b) *The SSSC codes of practice* [online] https://www.sssc.uk.com/about-us/publications/sssc-codes-of-practice-for-social-service-workers-and-employers-2024-version/.

SSSC (2024c) *Registration data: Current snapshot* [online] https://data.sssc.uk.com/registration-data#snapshot.

SSSC (2024d) *Registration is changing* [online] https://www.sssc.uk.com/the-scottish-social-services-council/registration-is-changing/.

SWS (2024) *What is SWEP* [online] https://socialworkscotland.org/sws-projects/social-work-education-partnership/#:~:text=Social%20Work%20Education%20Partnership%20(SWEP,social%20work%20education%20in%20Scotland.

Westwood, J, Pemble, C and Patterson, F (2016) *Leadership in social work qualifying education: A report for the review of social work* [online] https://www.sssc.uk.com/knowledgebase/article/KA-01882/en-us.

Chapter 2

The importance of learning in direct practice for social work

Introduction

This chapter explores the nature of how social workers learn in, through and at work, arguing that practice is a rich source of professional learning across career stages. Learning through practice is an integral element of qualifying programmes however not always fully recognised or valued by social workers or organisations beyond that stage. Understanding the complexity of learning in practice settings can help us rethink approaches to continuing professional learning (CPL) for social workers.

Chapter aims

By the end of the chapter, you will be able to:

- understand the relationship between practice and learning in social work;
- recognise the importance of learning in practice at all stages of your career;
- create a plan that integrates learning through practice in your role.

Learning in social work practice in Scotland

There are clear requirements in the Scottish education and post-qualifying learning standards for social workers which include practice learning; however, this is most explicit at the pre-qualifying stage. Social work draws from diverse conceptions and theories of learning to inform methods used to teach and develop practice which feature throughout this book. What is understood as learning is influenced by the way you understand the complex cognitive, physiological and social processes that are involved. What you, your organisation or the profession more broadly values as learning is also an important influence on how social workers learn. While there have been significant shifts in understanding learning as a continuum of informal and formal activities, a tension remains in that individuals and organisations continue to place emphasis on training and tangible outputs in what they plan and value (Gordon et al., 2019; Ferguson, 2022; McCulloch et al., 2024). Research from social workers in Scotland consistently reports that some of the most valuable learning for them has come from direct practice experiences (Grant et al., 2022: Ferguson, 2023; McCulloch et al., 2024). Learning from the lived experiences of social workers can help us understand just how complex and extraordinary learning is in practice settings. Before you are introduced to a model that

DOI: 10.4324/9781041057598-4

draws from this evidence, you can reflect on your own learning journey. If you are just starting out as a social work student, you can come back to reflect on these questions at any time on your journey.

Reflective questions

- What is the most important thing you have ever learned as a social worker?
- Where did you learn this?
- Why does this matter to you as a social worker?

Perhaps you identified something that has a personal connection or was linked with a specific case. The details of where and how you learned might have involved a practice situation. If you learned on a training course, there may have been a vital connection to your practice. You may not have noticed you were learning at the time but now recognise what you have done differently since. Understanding why your learning has been important will be related to you or your practice, and in many cases both. Research suggests that learning as a social worker is a deeply personal experience that integrates 'physical and emotional elements while navigating places, spaces and tasks' (Ferguson, 2023). The way in which learning and practice are intertwined is now considered.

Learning as practice

Social work is 'a practice-based profession', defined clearly as such by the International Federation of Social Workers (IFSW, 2014, p2). Practice learning for social work students forms an intensive and substantial part of qualifying training. Social work is a life-changing profession dealing with real people. Imagine what it would be like to qualify as a social worker without doing any practice in real-life situations. There are many things that can perhaps only ever be learned by being immersed in doing them through 'the art of practice' (Ferguson, 2021, p92). Social work practice is described as the 'crucible of learning' (Gould and Baldwin, 2004, p4) where different elements interact leading to the creation of something new.

When it comes to the complexity of the social work role (Hood, 2015), experience that helps you understand how theory, legislation and skills come to life in your interventions is essential. Learning through your relationships and communication with real people in practice is central to professional development throughout your career. Learning and practice 'are two sides of the same coin´ (Thompson, 2017, p2). Social workers must always start with practice (Thompson, 2017), retaining this at the core of subsequent analysis or theorising processes. Approaches to learning that centre the person in the process have developed well in social work in Scottish research. Collingwood et al.'s (2008) Theory Circle and models of reflective practice such as the Practice Pyramid (Gordon and Mackay, 2017) are rooted in practice. These approaches are extensively used by practice educators and practitioners across geographic and service settings and confirm the complexity of social work and the process of learning within the practice landscape. Practice is central to professional learning whether social workers are in the early stages of their career (McCulloch et al., 2024) or qualified for several decades (Ferguson, 2023).

Learning in practice

I don't think I've ever stopped learning. I wouldn't say I go home every day and say what I have learned that day but I am constantly learning. If you've come into contact with people, different ideas, different experiences, you learn from that and could be learning how to do things or how not to do things. I think I have probably learned those in pretty equal measures. I used to say to people, it'd be really good to be something like a joiner or a plumber that people could look at your work and tell you 'That's a really good job you've done there', they can see it. In social work it's seldom, it's never as clear cut as that is it?

(Karl in Ferguson 2021, p142)

What it is like learning in social work practice

Social workers develop their understanding of the enormity of their decisions and the impact of these on families in direct practice (Ferguson, 2021). The dynamic nature of tasks, *'keeping children alive and safe', 'trying to reduce chaos', 'trying to be realistic' and 'understanding risk'* are some specific examples of what qualified social workers have learned through their practice (Ferguson, 2021, p149). Practice settings are also the landscape in which diversity, power and privilege need to be explored in situated contexts. Awareness of your own identity, culture and background are an essential foundation for developing anti-oppressive practice that authentically facilitates social justice (Tedam, 2021). This is one example of the rich kinds of learning that direct practice offers for social workers. This is central to your own experiences and how you will negotiate ethical relationships with others.

Workplace learning as a complex web

Learning in any workplace is fundamentally different to learning in educational institutions (Billett, 2001). The learning environment will either promote or restrict learning according to whether it is expansive or restrictive in the practices encouraged (Engeström, 2008). It is therefore essential to understand the nature of the work and the place to support effective learning. Illeris (2011) helpfully demonstrates the complexity of workplace learning and the dynamic processes involved (Ferguson, 2022). Illeris suggests that an individual dimension that involves learning content, outcomes, motivations and learner volition interacts with an organisational dimension when work is taking place (Illeris, 2011). The organisational influences include the technical-rational and social-cultural environments of the workplace, nature of work, patterns of allocation, distribution and division of labour (Illeris, 2011). This means that learning is generated in the spaces where these dimensions come together.

Learning in the workplace is a complex web of multiple interwoven physical and emotional elements for social workers. Figure 2.1 shows a visual representation of what the structure and texture of social workers' experiences of workplace learning involves. The threads between different elements form a unique web for each social worker linked with their embodied experiences of learning and the type of work opportunities they undertake.

Journey of the self · Navigating landscape and place · Navigating tasks · Learning through the body

Learning though others · Practices and conceptions of learning · Learning by chance

Figure 2.1 Learning experiences as a complex web.

Interwoven elements of learning

The interwoven elements in Figure 2.1 are drawn from research with social workers in Scotland who provided rich, detailed accounts of what it is like to be learning in practice settings. The web shows that you are immersed in direct practice as a social worker, and often learning is closely related to your personal life, motivation, development of professional identity and your own values. Learning to use and manage self is also central to the trajectory of your learning from the early career stages onwards. Some social workers described creating a new persona to navigate the unknown terrain of practice where there was no route map:

> You've got a whole swathe of different professionals and people that you work with so that the way that I talk to the children's hearing and then present a case is different than when I do an unannounced visit to a family. All that screwing on a different head in the sense of recreating yourself.
>
> (Boab in Ferguson, 2021, p93)

In contrast, other social workers talked about integrating their private and professional selves 'like a ball with two bits that intertwine, that merging of your person coming together as a social worker. I think learning to be a social worker is learning to be you, but on a different level' (Caroline in Ferguson, 2021, p135).

Navigating the places and spaces where social work happens is also central to the learning process. Workplaces are diverse, sometimes physically or psychologically isolated; are inextricably associated with the task at hand and can be a person's home, the court, children's hearing or 'the sheriff's house in the middle of the night' (Ferguson, 2021, p109). Within diverse workplaces, the social work task is experienced as complex and ambiguous (Hood, 2015), with multiple layers and expectations from individuals, families, other professionals and the public. Learning in practice is acknowledged as essential for equipping social workers to have core skills, knowledge and values irrespective of setting (SSSC, 2024c).

Physical and emotional aspects of learning in practice

Sensory experiences in social workers' learning are definitive in providing a rationale for the importance of learning through practice. Social workers describe significant learning associated with the embodied and sensory aspects of practice, 'going in, in your own body', 'thinking through your senses…you can't pin it down to what you see, it's what you feel, what you smell' (Danny in Ferguson, 2021, p151). Specific learning points are associated with these sensory experiences; one social worker described 'life and death in the smell' of contrasting care environments and articulated career-long learning about trusting cues in practice assessing risk (Danny in Ferguson, 2021, p151). Emotional experiences are also central to the learning process. This includes a broad spectrum of practice learning to manage your own emotions and those of other people. Emotional intelligence is widely recognised as a core skill in social work (Ingram, 2013), with practice offering the opportunity to develop and demonstrate this.

Reflective questions

- Which emotional and/or physical aspects of learning through direct practice have you experienced?
- What way have these influenced your learning? What have you learned through these experiences?
- Has it been possible to share these aspects of learning in supervision, or with colleagues, and what were the benefits of this?

You might have thought about a range of work that has involved difficult emotional experiences, or perhaps a mixture of powerful, joyful examples of learning too. Difficult experiences may have been the focus of reflection or your supervision, and there were clear links to your learning, or in other scenarios, you might have reflected more privately on a complex situation. It is important to remember that you are an individual in how you learn, the way that practice is experienced by you and your learning style and preferences (see Chapter 4).

Learning in real life

In practice settings, everyone is a learner, whether they think so or not. Everyone is also an educator. The role of other people fundamentally shapes social workers' experiences of learning in practice. Direct practice affords the essential opportunity to learn from people that you are working with. Although there are many developments in practice simulation and use of practice scenarios to support learning in social work education, real encounters remain crucial to what and how social workers learn. Learning through others is discussed fully in the next sections of the book, including how you can learn from people using services, carers, your peers and other professionals.

Figure 2.1 also includes the concept of learning by chance as part of social workers' experiences. Social workers described some of their most significant learning experiences as being completely by chance (Ferguson, 2021). Chance variables include the paths that led to applying for specific jobs, where qualifying placements were, the specific cases allocated and who they were in teams with or managed by. Social workers discussed, 'it almost kind of depends on where you end up…who you surround yourself with and the kind of conversation you are willing to get into' (Chloe in Ferguson, 2021, p173).

Practice offers the opportunity to learn through watching, listening, demonstration and discussion. It is also the site of professional supervision. Practice tasks that are available and the way that these are allocated is a variable that organisations can review to support more consistent learning opportunities. In the chapter so far, you have explored some of the ways that practice is important for professional learning. Thinking about how this can be embedded in your approach to professional learning is relevant whether you are starting as a student or have many years of experience.

Learning through practice across the social work career

Practice features in social workers' learning at all stages of your career. Often the transitions in stages of your journey as a social worker are marked by milestones in your learning such as the assessment of you practice learning as a student or completion of the Newly Qualified Social Worker (NQSW) Supported Year in practice. There are ways that learning is supported in practice settings that span all stages, however learning can feel fundamentally different depending on whether you are being assessed, your experience of professional supervision or the nature of the learning culture in your workplaces. Standards relating to assessed practice days in pre-qualifying programmes, and the timeline of their revision, were outlined in Chapter 1. These form the most explicit requirements for integrating practice in the learning curriculum. An overview of the stages and transitions in social workers' careers with mapping to practice learning and CPL requirements is shown in Table 2.1 with key details about how learning is supported and/or assessed at these times.

In newly introduced Return to Practice Standards (SSSC, 2024d), supervised practice also forms a central part of CPL evidence for social workers who are returning to the social work register. An advanced practice framework (SPICe, 2022), shown in the timeline in Chapter 1, will articulate the characteristics of social workers, their skills and knowledge aligned with ethical principles embedded in pre-qualifying and NQSW frameworks for professional learning. More details are discussed in Part Two of this book along with how you can make your CPL personally meaningful for the whole of your career.

Commitment to learning from practice in Scottish social work

The Scottish Social Services Council (SSSC) has always recognised and encouraged practitioners to reflect on practice experiences as part of their CPL. SSSC regulatory guidance and information has continually strengthened the promotion of informal and workplace learning in the revision of the CPL requirements (SSSC, 2024c) and is fully embedded in the NQSW guidance for employers, supervisors and social workers (SSSC, 2024b). The aims of the CPL requirements for NQSW are 'to ensure consolidation and advancement of professional practice' (SSSC, 2024b, p17) through improved consistency of access to learning opportunities, support and professional supervision. Core learning elements

Table 2.1 Learning elements in social work career stages

Professional supervision, learning in direct practice, learning with others and critical reflection across all career stages

Student (pre-qualifying)

Formal requirements include a set minimum number of days in directly assessed practice in 'service delivery settings' (SSSC, 2024a).

Contrasting learning experiences are required.

Practice is assessed against the Standards in Social Work Education (SSSC, 2019).

Learning is formally supervised and assessed by a Practice Educator.

A named workplace supervisor may be identified if the Practice Educator is not on-site.

Newly qualified social worker (NQSW)

Transition from pre-qualifying stage should be supported and is set in regulatory requirements (SSSC, 2024b).

A framework for the NQSW Supported Year in Scotland integrates employer and practitioner expectations about CPL (SSSC, 2024b).

Core learning elements support professional development linked to learning in context of social work practice (SSSC, 2024b).

A comprehensive, integrated model of support includes professional supervision, protected learning time and protected case load (SSSC, 2024b).

Learning is verified by the supervisor within the practice setting.

Early-career social worker (ECSW)

Identified as a liminal and career transition stage in Scottish research (Grant et al., 2022).

Up to five years post-qualifying.

Social workers may or may not identify as ECSW at any time, shifting from NQSW to Social Worker identification.

No specific framework for supporting CPL but regulatory requirements to meet for continued registration (SSSC, 2024c).

Practice experience is recognised as opportunity for CPL.

Practice itself is not assessed unless undertaking a specialist accredited award.

Social worker (SW)

Social work identity continues to shape (Grant et al., 2022).

CPL requirements set by SSSC need to be met (SSSC, 2024c).

Practice experience is recognised as opportunity for CPL.

Practice itself is not assessed unless undertaking a specialist accredited award.

integrate 'knowledge, skills and value common to all professional social work practice irrespective of setting' (SSSC, 2024b, p3).

Crucially, the SSSC approach is informed by research into the lived experiences of social workers and an understanding of how they learn in practice (SSSC, 2024b). Specifically, the supporting principles cite 'evidence from learning from a range of formal, informal, and naturally occurring workplace learning and development opportunities' as the benchmark of what is valued (SSSC, 2024b, p9). There is a systematic sequence of support, review and validation of learning built into the first qualified period in practice in which professional supervision is the mainstay (SSSC, 2024b). Professional supervision provides a central function across the career as a developmental space within a 'rich, responsive and nurturing learning environment' (McCulloch et al., 2024, p19). Within this environment, knowledge is both generated and used. Organisations have a primary role in meeting the aims of the NQSW regulatory requirements with these relying on effective induction, protected learning time, protected caseload and professional supervision.

There are numerous texts written about practice learning which focus on the student, and to varying degrees the NQSW stages, but foregrounding practice learning is an exciting component of CPL throughout your career. Shared across all stages of CPL are the essential ingredients that come from the practice setting:

- professional supervision;
- peer support and shared learning;
- learning in and through practice;
- learning with and from people with lived experiences of social work services;
- encouragement of self-directed learning activities;
- critical reflection on use of self and analysis of practice;
- learning about the responsibility for promoting wellbeing and protection across the lifespan irrespective of role.

Learning in practice

It is that kind of subconscious bit that you're always kind of developing ways to do things in practice anyway and that then shapes what underpins your practice moving forward. I think you learn a lot when cases maybe don't go so well either it is the subconscious professional development that you do when you are working a case. I think if you don't have the time to think back on why you have done things or why things have worked you can just keep running with it and you would just go into the next thing without maybe understanding why that worked well or why the outcome was better than another time. I think having feelings and the emotional side of these things and then being able to reflect on why you felt that way and what triggered that, I think that then really kind of promotes your learning

(Sophie in Ferguson, 2021, p117)

Planning for learning in practice

In this chapter, you have explored evidence about learning through practice and been encouraged to think about the importance of this for all career stages. You will be able to focus on the specific stage you are at, or your areas of interest, in Part Two of this book. Planning for your CPL can ensure that you remember to include and value practice learning opportunities.

Reflective questions

- How can you maximise the opportunities to learn from and reflect on practice as part of learning?
- What are the opportunities to strengthen what you and your organisation do?
- Make a few notes and identify any actions.

Summary points

- Practice and learning are fundamentally linked in social work.
- Learning in the workplace is a complex personal process for social workers.
- Direct practice is central to CPL across the whole of your career.
- Organisations have a key role to foster learning in the workplace.

Further reading

A quick read

The importance of workplace learning for social workers is my quick summary published by Iriss in Scotland. This is helpful for social workers and their employers to support effective organisational practices for professional learning (Ferguson, 2022).

A helpful model

The theory circle is a firm favourite for exploring skills, values and knowledge in practice learning. You can read more about the development and use of Pat Collingwood, Ruth Emond and Rona Woodward's, *The Theory Circle: A Tool for Learning and for Practice* (Collingwood et al., 2008).

A deeper dive

If you are interested in workplace learning, you can read the groundbreaking work of Knud Illeris who has written magical and easily understandable theory in *The Fundamentals of Workplace Learning* (Illeris, 2011).

Please also see the resources section in the Appendix.

References

Billett, S (2001) 'Learning through work: Workplace affordances and individual engagement', *Journal of Workplace Learning*, 13(5/6): 209–214, https://doi.org/10.1108/EUM0000000005548.

Collingwood, P, Emond, R and Woodward, R (2008) 'The theory circle: A tool for learning and for practice', *Social Work Education*, 27(1): 70–83, https://doi.org/10.1080/02615470601141409.

Engeström, Y (2008) *From teams to knots: Activity-theoretical studies of collaboration and learning at work*, Cambridge University Press, Cambridge.

Ferguson, G (2021) *"When David Bowie created Ziggy Stardust" The lived experiences of social workers learning through work*, The Open University. https://doi.org/10.21954/ou.ro.0001306a

Ferguson, G (2022) *The importance of workplace learning for social workers* [online] www.iriss.org.uk/sites/default/files/2022-12/insights-67.pdf.

Ferguson, G (2023) '"When David Bowie created Ziggy Stardust" reconceptualising workplace learning for social workers', *The Journal of Practice Teaching and Learning: Papers from the International Conference on Practice Teaching and Field Education in Health and Social Work*, 20(1): 67–87.

Gordon, J and Mackay, G (2017) 'The practice pyramid: A model for integrating social work values, theory and practice', *Journal of Practice Teaching and Learning*, 14(3): 51–64, https://doi.org/10.1921/jpts.v14i3.1015.

Gordon, J, Gracie, C, Reid, M and Robertson, L (2019) *Post-qualifying learning in social work in Scotland: A research study* [online] https://mysssc.microsoftcrmportals.com/knowledgebase/article/KA-02685/en-us.

Gould, N and Baldwin, M (2004) *Social work, critical reflection and the learning organization,* Ashgate, Aldershot.

Grant, S, McCulloch, T, Daly, M and Kettle, M (2022) *Newly qualified social workers in Scotland: A five-year longitudinal study final report* [online] www.sssc.uk.com/knowledgebase/article/KA-03313/en-us.

Hood, R (2015) 'How professionals experience complexity: An interpretative phenomenological analysis', *Child Abuse Review*, 24(2): 140–152, https://doi.org/10.1002/car.2359.

IFSW (2014) *Global definition of social work* [online] www.ifsw.org/what-is-social-work/global-definition-of-social-work/.

Illeris, K (2011) *The fundamentals of workplace learning,* Routledge, London.

Ingram, R (2013) 'Locating emotional intelligence at the heart of social work practice', *British Journal of Social Work*, 43(5), 987–1004, https://doi.org/10.1093/bjsw/bcs029.

McCulloch, T, Grant, S, Daly, M, Sen, R and Ferguson, G (2024) 'Embedding learning as a practice of value: Learning from the experiences of early career social workers in Scotland', *The British Journal of Social Work*, 54(7): 2977–2995, https://doi.org/10.1093/bjsw/bcae072.

SPICe (2022) *Social work workforce FAQs* [online] spice-spotlight.scot/2022/05/30/social-work-workforce-faqs/.

SSSC (2019) *Standards in social work education* [online] learn.sssc.uk.com/siswe/.

SSSC (2024a) *Revised standards for teaching, learning and assessment,* Scottish Social Services Council, Dundee.

SSSC (2024b) *NQSW supported year overview and guidance 2024* [online] https://www.sssc.uk.com/about-us/publications/nqsw-supported-year-overview-and-guidance-2024/.

SSSC (2024c) *Continuous professional learning (CPL)* [online] www.sssc.uk.com/supporting-the-workforce/continuous-professional-learning/.

SSSC (2024d) *Introducing return to practice requirements for social workers* [online] at news.sssc.uk.com/news/return-to-practice-requirements-social-workers#:~:text=Following%20our%20consultation%20in%20autumn,effect%20from%203%20June%202024.

Tedam, P (2021) *Anti-oppressive practice,* Sage, London.

Thompson, N (2017) *Theorizing practice,* Second edition, Palgrave Macmillan, London.

Chapter 3

Leadership for social work learning in Scotland

Introduction

This chapter explores the individual, organisational and strategic opportunities for leading professional learning in Scottish social work, arguing that this must not be left to chance. The concept of a professional learning ecosystem for social work education and CPL is explored along with the key leadership attributes that are essential for it to flourish. Professional leadership is explored more broadly before identifying how individual and collective approaches can strengthen social work in Scotland.

Chapter aims

By the end of the chapter, you will be able to:

- describe the essential ingredients of effective leadership;
- understand the role of leadership for learning in Scottish social work;
- identify the opportunities you have as a leader to support learning.

Leadership and Scottish social services

Leadership theories and styles remain a topic at the fore of change processes across social services at all levels. A recent scoping report from Scotland confirms the contested nature of leadership but also highlights that social work leadership is a 'continuum, part of the necessary skills of the workforce, from student right through to Chief Social Work Officer' (Martin, 2024, p39). Models of leadership include classical approaches concerned with hierarchy, responsibility and accountability that are often transactional. Shared and distributed leadership models take a more transformative, adaptive approach and have been integrated into teaching about leadership in social work for many years. Distributed leadership and situated leadership (Hersey and Blanchard, 1993) shift from highly directive approaches to dynamic support along a continuum according to situations, highly relevant for the social work context. More information about leadership styles for those unfamiliar with these can be found in the recommended reading at the end of this chapter. Leadership development initiatives have been high on the national strategic agenda for several decades recognising the need for complex systems change.

The Scottish Social Services Council (SSSC) has directly responded to the leadership agenda in the development of an extensive suite of resources and long history of facilitating programmes in the sector. The Scottish Government has even been at the helm of

DOI: 10.4324/9781041057598-5

promoting 'new consciousness and a new collective leadership capacity' to promote sustainable societal change through Theory U (Scharmer, 2018). Scharmer integrates concepts from organisational learning, design thinking and emancipatory leadership in 'rethinking the parts and the whole by making it possible for the system to sense and see itself' (Scharmer, 2018, p17).

What is leadership?

Your view of leadership might be influenced by your previous experiences. The legacy of either inspirational or ineffective leaders can be equally strong in our perspectives of the skills and qualities we prioritise as important for leadership in social work.

Reflective questions

- Who has been an effective leader in your experience?
- What skills and qualities do you think are important for leaders?
- Do you see yourself as a leader?

Many social workers do not see themselves as leaders, and sometimes the best leaders do not recognise their influence. Acting with integrity, influencing good practice and promoting ethical rights-based practice are good examples of leadership qualities that are often associated with influential social workers. The influence of others on social workers' learning will be explored more fully in Chapter 9. Leadership capabilities have been defined as *Vision, Collaborating and Influencing; Empowering, Creativity and Innovation, Motivating and Inspiring* and *Self-Leadership* (SSSC, 2016). Such capabilities can be enhanced and developed across the workforce. It is essential to recognise that guiding, influencing and shaping good practice is a fundamental aspect of leadership in social work. This might take the form of supporting, representing or raising issues at an organisational or strategic level.

Having the confidence to represent and promote social work in interprofessional contexts is also a crucial high-stakes leadership task. There are many people driving social work issues in Scotland that you might think of as leaders. For example, Dr. Toyin Adenugba-Okpaje is Co-chair of the Scottish Association of Social Workers (SASW) and has been inspirational in her activism on anti-racism, practice expertise and support for the profession. Another example is that Billy Fisher from a local authority context has led workforce planning and professional practice issues for many years, chairing a national network for learning and development professionals. Social work has social justice as a core mission. Leadership for transformation and social justice therefore focuses on some of the most challenging issues that humans face.

Reflective questions

- What ways does leadership for learning contribute to social justice?
- In which specific issues does social work have a leadership role?
- How can social work as a profession strengthen leadership on these key agendas?

Social work strives to prevent and respond to individual and systemic harm. For example, anti-racist practice remains a critical issue for all social workers to understand and lead change. The climate ecological crisis has a disproportionate impact on those already affected by inequalities, including women, people living in poverty, people with disabilities, children and older people (UN, 2019), and is another complex issue for social work leadership (Ferguson and Giddings, 2025). While there is a clear mandate relating to the role of a social worker in responding to wellbeing, risk and harm, our personal decisions about how we lead learning and change will shape the future.

Citizen leadership

Citizen leadership has long been recognised in Scotland in relation to the skills of children, young people, adults and carers who are using social work services and involving them to make sure needs are met (Scottish Government, 2008). There are many people across all parts of the country who are in formal or informal leadership roles, often leading from within services, and we all have the potential to influence. Scharmer states that 'leadership is a distributive phenomenon. It needs to include all of us, it's not something we can delegate to the one person at the top' (2021).

Leadership is also fundamentally connected to learning, and supporting learning in any way is part of social work. It is essential that we turn to think about leadership *for learning*, albeit this is firmly rooted in the wider context of social services practice and the overarching challenges that exist.

Leadership and learning

The motivation to make a difference remains a key driver for social workers across the career; leadership in this context involves being an ethical compass, a trusted colleague or sounding board, offering peer support – part of the ecosystem that supports learning. As a leader, you have the power to create truly reflective, safe, shared spaces for learning where social workers are together. Often there are forums and events set up, but unstructured time together and places with other social workers within work lead to significant learning (Cabiati, 2017; Ferguson, 2023).

If we do indeed see learning as practice as suggested in Chapter 2, then strengthening professional learning must also strengthen the social work profession. Managers at any level are central to this because they directly influence the work tasks and learning opportunities. Many organisational approaches to leading learning begin with needs analysis-type approaches, however these rarely encompass the complexity of learning, learners, systems and their interdependencies (Kubiak, 2012). Chapter 2 explored how social workers' learning is particularly nuanced to the demands of their extraordinary roles. Kubiak suggests that leading learning means balancing needs and aspirations across intersecting individual, team and organisational domains. Chapter 4 explores the deeply personal learning trajectory of individual social workers which is entwined with personal experience and motivation. We ultimately need learning to result in safe and effective practice for people who are using social work services, but the process is undoubtedly transformative for social workers and their own lives too.

Learning and development in organisations

Learning and development (L&D) personnel have one of the most instrumental leadership roles in how social workers learn in Scotland. While there is an amazing network and tradition of practice, this landscape has evolved in response to changing organisations, public sector cuts and the integration of the specific social work L&D function into wider Human Resource (HR) teams in many local authorities. This means that HR practitioners are managing complex regulatory and professional interests of many diverse workforce groups. Historically, many L&D practitioners dealing with social work matters were qualified social workers which may not be the case in current organisational arrangements.

L&D practitioners also often hold responsibility for:

- coordinating and managing social work student practice learning;
- brokering plans with specific teams;
- supporting students, practice educators, link supervisors and the wider services;
- developing and maintaining links with multiple universities;
- commissioning post-qualifying accredited programmes;
- direct facilitation of learning sessions;
- managing the requirements of the Newly Qualified Social Worker (NQSW) Supported Year;
- supporting CPL for all social workers.

These L&D responsibilities regularly form part of a much wider professional role across services, workforce groups or specialist areas. As part of a governance context, HR has multiple responsibilities and considerable expertise which can support social work effectively. Understanding the nature of social work and managing professional interests, supervision and continuing learning are examples of what is essential to lead effectively. It is necessary to plan for supporting *professionals* as opposed to *employees* in this respect and meet social work specific needs in an interprofessional context. L&D expertise includes employee wellbeing, leadership development, coaching and mentoring, managing change and service redesign. Different configuration of organisational support for the social worker workforce across Scotland does, however, mean that understanding of professional issues and meeting the needs of social work services is inconsistent (Kettle *et al.*, 2016). Anyone involved in L&D in whatever shape has one of the most significant leadership roles for social workers' learning across the whole of their career.

Learning in practice

I think learning as a Social Worker has not always been prioritised and trainings available post qualification have often, to me, felt quite basic or one dimensional. There has been value in them in terms of networking and supporting multi-agency communication, which is important but I have wanted more knowledge, more understanding so I can undertake the assessments of need, of risk and to offer the best support possible. Resources play a significant impact on the space given to social workers to develop their learning. It is hard to take a day out to go on training when you have a service user in crisis for example. Also having time to read some research even if it is a summary of recent research is also hard to find when teams are busy and there is not enough staff in the team. Being able to stop, learn, reflect is an incredibly challenging task when you are feeling overwhelmed by the tasks in front of you, the lack of resources (i.e. other services, financial support for families) and the impact of the team or service culture.

(Anna, Practice Educator Central Scotland)

Leadership across the social work career

A fantastic mapping between the Standards in Social Work Education (SiSWE), ethical principles and leadership capabilities highlights how important leadership is from the student stage onwards (SSSC, 2020). This follows from the SiSWE themselves having been informed by Scottish research into leadership in qualifying social work education (Woodward et al., 2016). Self-leadership and promoting social justice are strong components embedded in the SiSWE.

In Scotland, standards for a supported year for NQSWs recently launched in which professional leadership; promoting wellbeing, support and protection; and advocating for human rights are central (SSSC, 2024). In terms of ethics and values, there is an expectation to 'challenge and work to reduce social injustice through knowledge and analysis of the impact of social and structural factors on the lives of people' (SSSC 2024, p5). The standards use the first person to highlight personal responsibility. In the NQSW Supported Year, one of eight core learning elements is professional leadership: 'develop personal and professional authority as a social worker including when working collaboratively across agency and professional boundaries' (SSSC, 2024, p19). The leadership component of the NQSW Supported Year has a strong range of activity in focus but does strongly highlight leadership for learning. This includes that the NQSW 'should promote the profession and good practice, taking responsibility for the professional learning and development of self and others' (SSSC, 2024, p19). Further to this, 'take an active role in professional meetings, networks and bodies to support own and others' learning and development' and 'understand my responsibility to seek, plan and undertake ongoing professional development' are detailed for NQSWs as part of leadership (SSSC, 2024, p19).

The SiSWE and NQSW Supported Year are designed to provide the foundations for developing leadership capability integrated in the social workers' role for the whole of their career. Post-qualifying programmes in supervision, management and leadership remain popular for social workers as part of their CPL in the sector. The fundamental ethos of practice learning qualifications in Scotland is leadership for learning. This is a core part of the curriculum in the specialist awards and reflects the intention of the suite of qualifications. Leadership for learning extends beyond the direct role of assessing social work students to supporting all learners within practice settings. This might include responding to the needs of learners at different levels, developing practice, generating feedback and evaluating learning in practice settings.

Within the Codes of Practice, the role of employers' leadership for learning in providing 'learning and development opportunities to enable workers to strengthen and maintain their skills, knowledge and practice' is prominent (SSSC, 2024, p24). This section of the Codes of Practice has a further seven subsections detailing how this ought to be actualised. Self-leadership of learning is also at the fore 'my continuous professional learning to improve my knowledge and skills and contribute to the learning and development of others' (SSSC, 2024, p15). Supporting the learning of others takes many forms including mentoring, sharing new ideas, helping resolve conflict, seeking feedback and enhancing own skills, and challenging oppressive systems and practices.

There is a requirement for every local authority to appoint a professionally qualified Chief Social Work Officer (CSWO) set out in Section 3 of the Social Work (Scotland) Act 1968. A range of duties are detailed in the legislation that embed governance and leadership of the delivery of safe, effective and innovative practice and professional learning. The CSWO is therefore key in promoting individual and organisational learning across the complex and diverse partnerships that characterise the landscape. A specific qualification programme at Scottish Credit and Qualifications Framework (SCQF) Level 11 has been running in Scotland since 2016 for CSWOs and those who are aspiring to become them. The Standards for CSWOs set by the SSSC underpin this qualification which are summarised by a Venn diagram that integrates modelling values, setting direction, achieving outcomes, self-leadership and working with others (SSSC, 2015). Section 3.2 notes the CSWO responsibility to 'take responsibility for ensuring that a learning culture is in place for the organisation' and 'demonstrate commitment to the learning and development of staff' as a core aspect of managing people (SSSC, 2015).

Figure 1.1 showed key players in the Scottish social work landscape. Universities are also crucial for effective leadership in the sector as shown in this diagram. Many people working in social work programmes within universities retain a passion for practice and hold significant expertise. It is essential that we do not forget or fragment our shared interests and collective expertise in shaping leadership for the future of social work in Scotland.

A professional learning ecosystem for Scotland

Leadership in social work needs to be 'exercised at all levels and all need to pull together to ensure a strong Social Work profession for the future' (Daniel and Scott, 2018, p19). The complex adaptive system of social work means that there are multiple influencers on learning and multiple people in key roles – with opportunities to drive and support learning. Social work thinks systemically and uses ecological theories in relation to many areas of practice yet an overarching, connected approach to professional learning has been elusive in Scotland. In fact, social workers described their most significant learning experiences as being completely by chance in recent research (Ferguson, 2023). In any complex adaptive system, the focus needs to shift from the responsibility for learning at the individual level to a focus on the organisational context, culture and processes (Munro, 2020).

A learning ecosystem is a system of people, content, technology, culture and strategy with many connections and feedback loops that enable growth (Jackson, 2019). In any eco-system, the fundamental interdependencies between parts and the whole are crucial. Jackson suggests that a human community is a special kind of ecosystem, and it is our behaviour within this that matters. The nature of relationships and connections across the social work landscape are central to this. The dynamics of such an ecosystem 'depends not just on the principles that govern the flow of matter and energy...but also on what those flows mean for us' (Jackson, 2019, p3). We need to conceptualise the system to acknowledge the energy, expertise and potential of the people and relationships within it. Calls for an 'integrative, developmental and ecological approach to professional learning' (McCulloch et al., 2024, p1) are rooted in the experience of social workers in Scotland. McCulloch et al. also remind us of the disconnect between our research, knowledge, practice and policy, which means that attempts to develop in one part of the ecosystem undermine another. Why this remains such a wicked issue (Grint, 2008) is the business of us all. We need to think about the opportunities we have to influence these from whatever role we occupy. Martin suggests that 'there need to be concurrent interventions that support the whole system sustainably; governance/structures, recruitment/retention, training, leadership, improvement, and culture cannot be tackled in isolation' (Martin, 2024, p40).

Systems thinking embraces effective leadership theory, strategy and practice that agitates collective action for change. The collective consciousness needs to shift from ego-system awareness (silo) to eco-system awareness (Scharmer, 2018) if we are to develop better connectedness. Scharmer suggests that the 'essence of leadership is about the capacity of the system in which everyone is participating, to sense and shape the future' (Scharmer, 2021). The most effective leadership approach may be of systems conveners, those who are visionary, acting beyond silos on sustainable change, 'enabling learning in multi-stakeholder, multi-scaled and multi-practiced situations' (Wenger-Traynor and Wenger-Traynor 2021, p8) in response to the ultimate wicked issues associated with social work practice.

Learning in practice

Thinking about the web of workplace learning, there is almost another web that sits around that...It's those connections and all these roles and what you see as being your responsibility and your reach within that. We always encourage newly qualified workers to remember they are bringing something with them, it is not all one-way traffic. So, you try and build it within teams and then kind of wider within the organisation and the rest of it but I think that's a tricky thing to do when people are under a lot of pressure. There are multiple layers that enable learning in the web, there are a range of push and pull variables.

(Social worker, strategic leadership role)

Reflective questions

- Who is responsible for professional learning?
- What are your opportunities to lead learning for social workers? How might others use you as a role model?
- How would you visualise a cohesive, effective professional learning ecosystem for social work in Scotland?

Summary points

- Everyone can be a leader in social work.
- Developing leadership capabilities is part of social workers' learning and development.
- A vibrant professional learning ecosystem for social work involves connections across people and systems that are encouraged to flourish.
- Leadership for learning is where energy, skills, experience and support are fed into the ecosystem at any level.

Further reading

A quick read

For a recent summary based on Scottish focus groups, Hannah Martin's *Leadership in Social Work* report for Iriss gives a great snapshot and continues the call to action. A helpful summary of different leadership approaches and precis of theory are also included.

A helpful set of resources

An amazing array of current, relevant curated activities and resources can be found in the SSSC's fabulous '23 Things Leadership – Activities to support your leadership development in social and health services'. Created by inspirational learning and development advisors from SSSC and rooted in real-world Scottish social work expertise, '23 Things Leadership' is relevant for us all.

A deeper dive

If you are interested in creative ideas and really want to think differently about change, Otto Scharmer's work 'Leading for the Emerging Future' is a must. You can explore ideas about Theory U on the dedicated website https://www.presencing.org/theoryu or read *The Essentials of Theory U: Core Principles and Applications* which is what distils all of the research and materials found in Otto Scharmer's seminal texts *Theory U* and *Leading from the Emerging Future.*

   Please also see the resources section in the Appendix.

References

Cabiati, E (2017) 'What would you learn to improve your work in child protection? Social workers' continuing education requests', *Social Work Education*, 36(3): 257–272, https://doi.org/10.1080/02615479.2016.1269159.

Daniel, B and Scott, J (2018) *50th Anniversary: Social Work (Scotland) Act 1968* [online] https://socialworkscotland.org/projects/50th-anniversary-1968-social-work-scotland-act/.

Ferguson, G (2023) '"When David Bowie created Ziggy Stardust" reconceptualising workplace learning for social workers', *The Journal of Practice Teaching and Learning: Papers from the International Conference on Practice Teaching and Field Education in Health and Social Work*, 20(1): 67–87.

Ferguson, G and Giddings, L (2025) 'Social work practice, professional standards and the climate emergency: Opportunities for action', *Practice*, 1–19, https://doi.org/10.1080/09503153.2025.2505433.

Grint, K (2008) 'Wicked problems and clumsy solutions', *Clinical Leader*, 1(2): 54–68.

Hersey, P and Blanchard, K (1993) *Management of organizational behavior: Utilizing human resources*, Sixth edition, Prentice-Hall, Englewood Cliffs.

Jackson, N (2019) *Exploring learning ecologies,* Second edition [online] https://www.lifewideeducation.uk/uploads/1/3/5/4/13542890/lulu_upload.pdf.

Kettle, M, McCusker, P, Shanks, L, Ingram, R and McCulloch, T (2016) *Integrated Learning in Social Work: A review of approaches to integrated learning for social work education and practice*, Scottish Social Services Council, Dundee.

Kubiak, C (2012) 'Understanding support worker learning: Practice, participation and identity', PhD Thesis, The Open University, https://doi.org/10.21954/ou.ro.0000d5a3.

Martin, H (2024) *Leadership in social work* [online] https://www.iriss.org.uk/sites/default/files/2024-02/iriss-sws-leadership-social-work.pdf.

McCulloch, T, Grant, S, Daly, M, Sen, R and Ferguson, G (2024) 'Embedding learning as a practice of value: Learning from the experiences of early career social workers in Scotland', *The British Journal of Social Work*, 54(7): 2977–2995, https://doi.org/10.1093/bjsw/bcae072.

Munro, E (2020) *Effective child protection*, Third edition, Sage, London.

Scharmer, O (2018) *The essentials of theory U: Core principles and applications*, Berrett-Koehler, Oakland.

Scharmer, O (2021) *To change a system you have to have the courage to step into the unknown*, *EPALE Interview* [online] https://epale.ec.europa.eu/en/blog/epale-interview-otto-scharmer-change-system-you-have-have-courage-step-unknown.

Scottish Government (2008) *Citizen leadership happens when citizens have power, influence and responsibility to make decisions*, Scottish Government, Edinburgh.

SSSC (2015) *Standard for chief social work officers* [online] https://www.sssc.uk.com/about-us/publications/standard-for-chief-social-work-officers-2015/.

SSSC (2016) *Enabling leadership* [online] https://www.sssc.uk.com/knowledgebase/article/KA-02257/en-us.

SSSC (2020) *Developing your leadership as a social work student* [online] https://stepintoleadership.info/assets/pdf/SiSWE%20and%20Leadership.pdf.

SSSC (2024) *NQSW supported year overview and guidance 2024* [online] NQSW Supported Year: Overview and Guidance - SSSC NQSW website.

UN (2019) *Climate change recognized as 'threat multiplier', UN Security Council debates its impact on peace* [online] https://news.un.org/en/story/2019/01/1031322.

Wenger-Traynor, E and Wenger-Traynor, B (2021) *Systems convening a crucial form of leadership for the 21st century* [online] https://www.wenger-trayner.com/wp-content/uploads/2021/09/Systems-Convening.pdf.

Woodward, J, Pemble, C and Patterson, F (2016) *Leadership in social work qualifying education*, Scottish Social Services Council, Dundee.

Part Two

Learning in the social work landscape

Chapter 4

Preparing for learning as a social worker

Introduction

This chapter considers ways of preparing psychologically and practically for social work practice. Preparation is often explored when students are getting ready for and being assessed in substantive assessed practice placements, however this is central to social work throughout the career. Tasks, roles and the expectations of practice require social workers to develop multifaceted resilience. This chapter explores social workers' experiences of how practice expectations fit with their personal values, motivation and readiness at different career points. Skills for learning self-awareness, emotional intelligence and use of self are also considered. Developing social work identity is another important aspect of professional development alongside balancing professional practice with personal lives. This chapter considers the emotional and physical aspects of social workers' learning experiences acknowledging the deeply personal journey that they take throughout their careers.

Chapter aims

By the end of the chapter, you will be able to:

- describe the personal journey of becoming a social worker;
- understand how to prepare for social work practice throughout your career;
- identify key areas for self-development as part of your learning.

What do we mean by preparing for social work practice?

The Standards in Social Work Education (SiSWE) clearly position preparation for practice right at the start of Standard 1, a clear focus, often discussed in relation to social work student activities prior to and within assessed placements. It is expected that readiness to practice is also assessed in all approved programmes. Standard 1 encompasses a range of elements that set the foundation for social work practice including practical preparation, ethics and professional integrity, working with other professionals, engaging with people to promote social justice and understanding people in the context of their lives. These are just some examples of the breadth of Standard 1 which set the tone for engaging with people, considering risk and challenging oppression, themes which then develop across the SiSWE and into the Newly Qualified Social Worker (NQSW) Supported Year in Practice.

DOI: 10.4324/9781041057598-7

For example, Core Learning Element 1 in the NQSW Supported Year cites that 'NQSWs will continue to develop a strong ethical base that emphasises the importance of building a positive, professional relationship with people' (SSSC, 2024, p5). Codes of Practice for Social Services Workers embed personal responsibility for learning, preparation for practice and wellbeing (SSSC, 2024).

Ethical foundations

Ethical Principles are shared across the expectations of the student, NQSW and Continuing Professional Learning (CPL) stages demonstrating their importance as a consistent underpinning area of development for social workers. They concern themselves with the values, attitudes and behaviours of social workers and recognition of dynamic use of self 'maintaining personal and professional boundaries, honesty, responsible confidentiality management and not abusing the trust of people receiving services. This also means taking responsibility for making ethical and evidence-informed decisions and being accountable for actions' (SSSC, 2019, p31). Gordon and Dunworth (2016) demonstrate that the use of self has fluctuated in the Scottish social work context over time, but this is key in current standards. To be able to effectively use and manage self requires understanding and awareness, a prerequisite for social work practice across the career. The concept of preparation therefore extends far beyond common presumptions of reading over case notes and planning a practical task. Preparing for what social work involves is relevant no matter how long someone has been a social worker and includes being ready for the task itself but also being personally prepared for the role.

A deeply personal journey

One of the main themes within the lived experiences of social workers was described as the *Journey of the self*, a deeply personal and unique learning journey (Ferguson, 2021). Some social workers think that it is actually very difficult to prepare for the uncertainty of many situations: 'How do you prepare?', 'What might work for one person would not work for another person' and 'What you learn to do in one situation won't necessarily help you in another' (Ferguson, 2021, p260). This is not a deficit in professionals, simply a marker of the complexity of their tasks. Grant *et al.* (2022) and McCulloch *et al.* (2024) show that social workers experience a duality of readiness at the early career stages – feeling ready and unready in equal measure. Ferguson (2021) also found that social workers, some with careers spanning as much as 40 years, could feel unprepared for dynamic, unpredictable and extraordinary tasks. Social workers are immersed in practice in which their personal values, motivation, previous experiences from life and work all combine in their development as a professional. Understanding yourself, your learning needs and how your lived experiences influence your responses are an important part of preparation. Figure 4.1 shows an example of one social worker's learning experience, revealing the multiple and interrelated aspects of what this has involved for them. The image is drawn from research that encapsulated individual learning experiences in a web to represent all the components.

Carol's experience of learning as a social worker depicts a web of interwoven parts of her learning experiences that comprise the whole. In the middle section, *self in situation*,

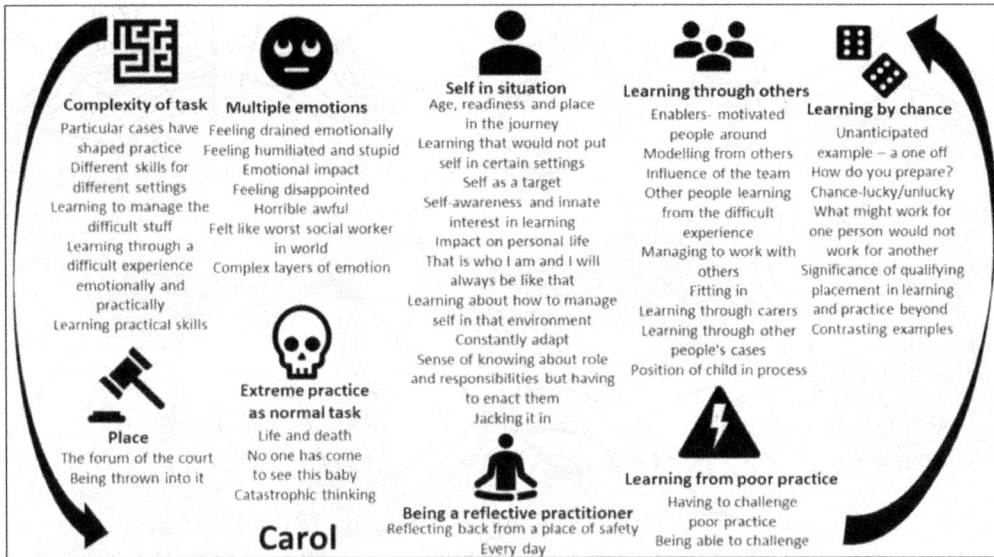

Figure 4.1 Carol's experience of learning as a social worker (Ferguson, 2021, p83).

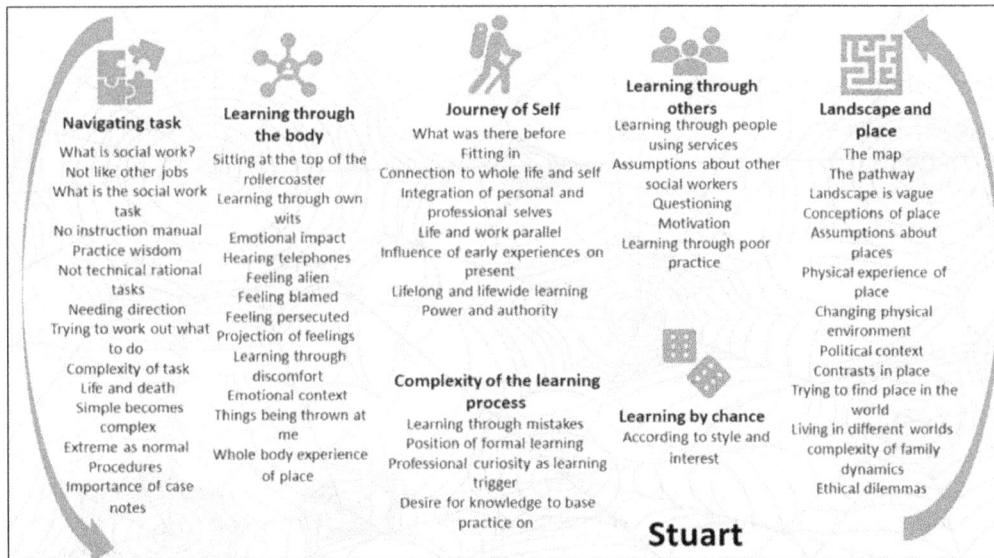

Figure 4.2 Stuart's experience of learning as a social worker (Ferguson, 2021, p99).

Carol identifies connections between her personal life with her professional development, her self-awareness, use of self in the practice context and her understanding of her role. Figure 4.2 depicts Stuart's learning experiences from the same research (Ferguson, 2021), again the personal journey features at the heart of professional learning but in a different configuration of elements.

Both Carol and Stuart include the paths that led them into social work as part of their overall journey. This includes where they have previously undertaken practice placements, previous employment and in Stuart's experience a sense of *fitting in* and finding a place that felt like a good alignment with his personal values echoed in other social workers' accounts. These ideas are closely linked with the notion of navigating the ethical areas of practice and where there were dilemmas around fairness, social justice or meaningful work (Ferguson, 2021).

If you are interested in exploring more of the images created in this research, there is a downloadable version resource available (Ferguson, 2023).

Reflective questions

- Why are you motivated to be a social worker?
- How has your personal journey linked with your professional learning?
- What ways have you found helpful to prepare for practice?

It is likely that your reflections on your journey are unique. Your experience may have been of having a strong drive to make a difference, to challenge oppression and disadvantage or to help with specific issues related to your lived experience. Alternatively, you may have taken a pragmatic decision to enter the profession for other reasons. Often there will be multiple motivating factors that bring social workers into and keep them in the profession (Giddings, 2024).

An evolving professional identity

Scottish social workers have produced a broad body of literature on the topic of social work identity, for example, Stephen Webb's edited volume on the subject (Webb, 2016) and Maura Daly's work (e.g., Daly *et al.*, 2024). Professional identity is a central aspect of continuing learning for social workers and remains hard to articulate (Wiles and Vicary, 2019). Some social workers describe the creation of a new persona to navigate social work practice, and others describe an integration of the personal and professional selves (Ferguson, 2021).

Learning in practice

When David Bowie created Ziggy Stardust it was about assuming someone else, now you can never escape yourself, but certainly you do assume different characters for different people that you work with. You've got judges and sheriffs you know so you've got a whole swathe of different professionals and people that you work with so that the way that I talk to the children's hearing and then present a case is different than when I go around and do an unannounced visit to a service user's family...all that screwing on a different head ...in the sense of recreating yourself ... there is a similarity there in ...social work ... that you need to be able to wear different hats for different audiences....

(Boab in Ferguson, 2021, p84)

> it's trying to separate [personal and professional] when coming together as a social worker with your morals and values every day but being able to separate them in cases like this to protect yourself. I think maybe it's trying to bring the profession and the person into one. There are layers of your professional self when you are together. I feel I've maybe got a little bit better, just about being more me than social worker if that makes sense, sometimes I think learning to be a social worker is learning to be you but on a different level.
>
> (Caroline in Ferguson, 2021, p121)

Caroline describes a very different process of becoming a social worker, integrating personal and professional selves 'like a ball with two bits that intertwine' (Caroline in Ferguson, 2021, p121). In relation to professional learning, this means for Caroline developing ways to manage social work practice and being able to 'put that hat down and have that personal life' (Caroline in Ferguson, 2021, p121). These different accounts from social workers tune into the significance of the self in professional practice, and preparing for this aspect of social work can be helpful. Professional identity is complex and only one part of the journey of self. Understanding who you are as a person, as a professional and as a learner will be a core part of CPL.

Understanding yourself as a learner

Social work practice educators will learn about the principles of Andragogy (Knowles, 1984), how adults learn in a way that is different to children with associated implications for teaching practices. Ideas about effective facilitation of learning and supportive environments are the subject of Part Three. Learner motivation, explored earlier in the chapter, is one important factor in adult learning. It is essential that learning has a relationship to what matters to the learner and a practical outcome for their practice. Social work students do not arrive as a blank slate; they come from all walks of life with associated experiences from life and work. It is common in social work education and in the practice learning stage to explore your learning styles and preferences. This is important to do whether as an educator and as a learner to consider what will enable you to learn most effectively. Awareness of your learning style and any specific needs or reasonable adjustments that will help you learn is also essential to negotiate with those that you are learning with.

Learning styles

Some of the common tools used to consider ways of learning are the Learning Styles Inventory (Honey and Mumford, 2006) or the Working Styles Questionnaire (Hawkey and Borkowski, 2003). Another popular learning-style typology VARK (Visual-Auditory-Read/Write-Kinesthetic) is often used to explore learner differences and preferences. There is no exact science on any of these approaches to understanding learners and in fact many critiques of the whole concept (e.g., Newton, 2015), including that they are rooted in

Western psychological perspectives. It is, however, important to think about how you learn and essential to reflect on what this means for your learning or the learners you are supporting. There are some great resources explaining learning styles and integrating these into supervision of learning in Scottish Social Services Council (SSSC, 2024) if you have not encountered these before.

There is a dynamic relationship between learners and educators within which our different experiences and expectations have a strong influence on learning outcomes. In the same way that social workers will consider the context of a person's life and the relationship to presenting issues, our learning is connected to our wider experience of previous education and our identity.

Learner differences

Aspects of identity including race, culture, age and socio-economic status are likely to be relevant to how we learn and what matters for learning relationships to flourish. You might find that this is explored at the start of your university studies or when you commence practice learning placements, but we need to continue to be aware of how we learn. The MANDELA model for practice learning (Tedam, 2013) is used extensively to support attention to the dynamics of relationships and individual learning needs. The acronym MANDELA encompasses Make Time, Acknowledge Need, Differences, Educational Experiences, Life Experiences and Age (Tedam, 2013), and encourages awareness of how these influence our learning and teaching practices.

Neurodiversity is also central to consider for practice learning (Thompson et al., 2024). Social work seeks to be inclusive, anti-oppressive and specifically anti-racist; therefore, our approaches to supporting professional learning must model this in an authentic way. Understanding about neurodiversity is a fast-developing area in social work and in education (Guthrie and Solomon, 2024), and we are learning increasingly from people's lived experiences of being neurodiverse (Green, 2020). It is important to explore what ways any neurodiverse learners need adjustments in social work practice learning arrangements, support and supervision. The neurodiverse learner is being assessed as well as managing learning and practice. It may be that new mechanisms are needed and/or additional support, compared to other settings they have been learning or working in (Open University, 2024).

Reflective questions

- Identify the ways that your styles will help or hinder your own learning.
- How might your learning style help or hinder learning of others?
- What is important for you to share about yourself for others to support your learning?

If you are an educator, you will also reflect on how you can gather information about people's learning needs to support them. One of the central messages of any theory around learning styles is that these are not a static, fixed position. It is suggested that through awareness of our own style, we can develop a plan to strengthen areas that are less comfortable for us and enhance our capacity for learning. It is also essential for you to think about what is important to communicate about your learning needs in terms of neurodiversity or disability. What kind of information will be important for lecturers, practice educators or colleagues to know to support your learning. Self-awareness is a key part of your preparation for social work professional development. Understanding and managing the complexity of practice is also essential. Reflection is a key feature of practice, introduced from early stages of social work education and highlighted as a core component of CPL across the career.

Reflection as professional learning

Reflective practice is never far from discussion when learning and development are discussed. Reflection is embedded in training and education across the profession, and understanding what this means as part of social work is central to preparation. Critical thinking is closely associated with reflective practitioners. Experiential learning has essential reflective processes represented as a four-stage cycle of experiencing, reflecting, thinking and acting (Kolb, 1984). Essentially, learning from practice comes from thinking and reviewing that experience and applying new knowledge, skills or approaches in subsequent situations. Although this sounds simple, many social workers find this hard to do. Reflection-for-action, Reflection-in-action and Reflection-on-action are suggested as distinct components of how reflection informs the whole learning process (Thompson and Thompson, 2023, p12). Reflection is associated with learning about self, appreciating different perspectives, emotional intelligence, understanding power dynamics, developing an anti-oppressive approach and managing ethical dilemmas.

Jennifer Moon has written prolifically around reflection for professional development for readers who want to explore more. Practical tools for reflective practice and integration of knowledge such as the Practice Pyramid (Gordon and Mackay, 2017) and the Theory Cycle (Collingwood *et al.*, 2008) draw directly from the experiences of social workers. Maclean *et al.* (2018) also offer the SHARE model which integrates the importance of Seeing, Hearing, Action, Reading and Evaluation connected to deep critical reflection. These are all helpful because there is a recognition of the complexity of reflective learning in the specific social work context.

Learning in practice

I think if you don't have the time to think back on why you have done things or why things have worked you can just keep running with it and you would just go into the next thing without maybe understanding why that worked well or why the outcome was better than another time. I think having feelings and the emotional side of these things and then being able to reflect on why you felt that way and what triggered that, I think that then really kind of promotes your learning to be able to take that forward.

(Sophie in Ferguson, 2021, p117)

Emotions and the body

Social workers' learning involves physical and emotional experiences. Sensory experiences of sight, smell, sound, touch and taste characterise rich descriptions of how social workers learn in extreme situations and extraordinary work. Corporeality (how we experience the world through the body) is one of the 'universal themes of life' (van Manen, 2014, p302), and yet learning through the body is a profound and surprising aspect of professional learning for social workers. Social work is not often associated with physical labour, which means the body can be ignored in practice, learning and education. While emotions and emotional labour (Hochschild, 1983) are more widely acknowledged, connections with physical feelings and sensations also need appreciated as part of how learning happens through social work practice.

Barnacle (2009) highlights embodied knowing as the integration of knowing, acting and being in a whole person. The body is the vehicle through which social workers practice and through which they learn. Often associated with physical and psychological isolation, social workers reveal 'you're just going in, in your own body' into situations where other professionals worked in pairs (Ferguson, 2021, p164). Both physical and psychological threads of social workers' experiences are directly linked with specific people, places and tasks. Intuitive practice and tacit knowledge are associated with the idea of gut instinct or hunches in social work. With the body present in all encounters, the gut is identified as having a central role in 'orientating thought', what a person pays attention to and what they subsequently do (Barnacle, 2009, p24).

Taking care of ourselves

Social workers also describe the impact of learning about the serious nature of the work and sense of responsibility (Ferguson, 2021). This includes developing awareness of power and authority in the social work task and role. Awareness of legal powers to restrict liberty, or remove children from their birth parents has also been part of learning. Learning to look after self and develop resilience is also a huge priority in social work and a key part of preparation (Kinman and Grant, 2020). The concept of self-care is suggested to have a multiplicity of meanings integral rather than peripheral to social work that are 'routinely categorised as an individual responsibility rather than being located in a structural framework shaped by factors including political ideology, funding, organizational culture, power, and discrimination' (Rose et al., 2025, p2). This reveals that self-care and conceptions of resilience are far from simple but are essential in any discussion relating to the social work profession. Often associated with reducing stress and burnout, Rose et al. provide evidence from the literature that self-care is also inextricably linked with social justice, rooted in a deeply political context. We cannot therefore divorce approaches to self-care from the experiences of social workers in the social conditions and pressures that they inhabit and which shape practice demands and responses. Self-care is seen to be central to effective and ethical social work practice, in terms of 'empathy, emotional awareness, reflexivity, and anti-oppressive practice' (Rose et al., 2025, p14).

Preparing for learning in social work practice involves integrating actions that will monitor and support social workers in their reflection and care. A focus on trauma-informed practice highlights this for practitioners and those they are working with alike (Scottish Government et al., 2023). This is embedded in standards and frameworks across career stages, however it comes in as a high priority in the NQSW Supported Year. Resources for employers, supervisors and NQSWs focus on resilience and self-care (although resource constraints in the sector continue to influence how well this can be actualised in the profession) (Grant et al., 2022). Our collaboration will be essential to continue to focus on looking after ourselves and others as an integral part of our professional practice into the future.

Getting prepared for learning

There are a few important practical issues highlighted here for professional learning and preparing for social work.

Engagement in professional supervision

From the practice learning stages of social work degrees, engagement in professional supervision forms an important part of how you reflect, review practice and assess your own professional development. Social work often cites supervision as a distinct aspect within the professional culture. Although supervision has many functions, learning and development are central and some excellent resources can be found for social workers and for supervisors on the dedicated NQSW website developed by the SSSC.

Developing critical thinking

A practical aspect of preparation for learning as a social worker involves getting ready for the academic requirements of study, if you are about to start your qualification. Social work programmes are designed to build knowledge in line with the Scottish Credit and Qualifications Framework (SCQF), demonstrating increased levels of reflection, applied theory and critical analysis over the course of your study. It is no surprise that there is a focus on developing criticality and applied use of theory within social work programmes, however this remains central to CPL.

Use of theories and other evidence to inform practice

This book does not seek to focus on the theories, evidence and research that should inform social work practice, but this is essential for learning. Josie Vallely developed an excellent creative tool called Navigating Evidence (Vallely, 2020), which enables social workers to explore sources of evidence that inform practice. Starting with the person is at the heart of applying knowledge to help understand and to intervene (Thompson, 2017).

Developing professional authority and decision-making

The idea of learning how to make a case, verbal and written reports and decision-making, is woven throughout social workers' experiences of learning in their practice (Ferguson, 2021). Skills for this aspect of practice are essential, embedded in the SiSWE, and involve the development of professional authority, accountability and demonstrable critical analysis that inform any recommendation. Scottish social work has a great range of published material on decision-making (e.g., Helm and Roesch-Marsh, 2017; Helm, 2022). NQSWs (Grant et al., 2022), those qualified beyond that phase (Ferguson, 2021) and Chief Social Work Officers (CSWOs) (Armstrong and Kettle, 2024) all report on the complexity, weight of responsibility and challenges in social work practice. Social workers in the most senior of roles are still grappling with and learning from practice experiences where they highlight 'isolation and vulnerability' (Armstrong and Kettle, 2024, p11). CSWOs are also highly reliant on 'good quality information from other social workers' (Armstrong and Kettle, 2024, p11).

Writing as social work practice

Writing for academic study, writing reflectively on practice and professional writing in social work are all core skills that often need development (Rai *et al.,* 2025). Writing for academic study will involve drawing together use of theory, evidence and critical thinking to demonstrate your understanding. Reflective writing takes many forms and will focus on thoughts, feelings, self-awareness and how these have influenced your practice. Careful reflection on the micro-skills you have used will also identify what has worked well or otherwise in practice situations. Writing in practice is doing social work; it is not a separate activity, but it is how social workers enact their values, records, recommendations and decisions (Rai *et al.,* 2025). Significant developments in Artificial Intelligence (AI) and Machine Learning have represented challenges for all types of social work writing with guidance for the profession imminent. Authentic, individual applied reflective writing that demonstrates your understanding simply can't be generated by AI. While there are undoubted opportunities for technology-enhanced writing, ethics, privacy and the sensitivity of social work data are paramount.

Reflective questions

- How will you prepare for the emotional and physical elements of learning?
- Who will be able to support you in your journey?
- Make a few notes and identify any actions.

Summary of key points

This chapter has explored the importance of preparation and ideas of readiness for social work practice. Preparation has been identified as essential for all career stages, not only in the student phase of social workers' professional development. Understanding yourself and your learning style is a prerequisite for engaging with others. Ethical foundations are at the heart of social work learning and practice. Practical preparation is important for all practice, however preparing emotionally for the journey of social work is also significant.

Further reading

A quick read

Sarah Rose's Iriss Insight on *Creating a culture of resilience for social workers* is a great quick read. If you are interested in self-care in social work, the journal article by Rose *et al.* (2025) is also recommended.

A helpful set of resources

A favourite of students, social workers and educators alike are Siobhan Maclean's *Theory Cards* (https://siobhanmaclean.co.uk/publications/social-work-theory-cards) and *Reflective Practice Cards* (https://siobhanmaclean.co.uk/publications/reflective-practice-cards) along with many online resources.

A deeper dive

Social Work: An Introduction edited by the wonderful team of Joyce Lishman, Janine Bolger, Neil Gibson, Gary Spolander and Chris Yuill now in its third edition has chapters across theory, intervention and practice contexts with learning resources woven throughout. A bonus is that it relates the content to the SiSWE.

Please also see the resources section in the Appendix.

References

Armstrong, T and Kettle, M (2024) 'My decision making is much more deliberate... I'm still energised by it: Lessons learned from the design and delivery of a module on judgement and decision making for senior social work managers', *Social Work Education*, 1–17, https://doi.org/10.1080/02615479.2024.2420668.

Barnacle, R (2009) 'Gut instinct', Chapter 2, in Dall' Alba, G (ed) *Exploring education through phenomenology: Diverse perspectives*, Wiley-Blackwell, United Kingdom, pp. 16–27.

Collingwood, P, Emond, R and Woodward, R (2008) 'The theory circle: A tool for learning and for practice', *Social Work Education*, 27(1): 70–83.

Daly, M, McCulloch, T and Smith, M (2024) 'The place of knowledge in constructing social work identity: Validating vagueness', *The British Journal of Social Work*, 54(3): 958–997, https://doi.org/10.1093/bjsw/bcad212.

Ferguson, G (2021) *"When David Bowie created Ziggy Stardust" the lived experiences of social workers learning through work*. The Open University [Online] https://oro.open.ac.uk/77930/.

Ferguson, G (2023) *Workplace learning for social workers: Learning in an incredible profession to do an extraordinary job*, The Open University, https://doi.org/10.21954/ou.ro.00104377.

Giddings, L (2024) 'Understanding how people stay in child and family social work roles – A work in progress', *Social Work Interpretative Phenomenological Analysis (SWIPA) Research Network Symposium 2024*, 11 Oct 2024 [online] https://oro.open.ac.uk/100751/.

Gordon, J and Dunworth, M (2016) 'The fall and rise of 'use of self'? An exploration of the positioning of use of self in social work education', *Social Work Education*, 36(5): 591–603, https://doi.org/10.1921/jpts.v14i3.1015.

Gordon, J and Mackay, G (2017) 'The practice pyramid: A model for integrating social work values, theory and practice', *Journal of Practice Teaching and Learning*, 14(3): 51–64, https://doi.org/10.1921/jpts.v14i3.1015.

Grant, S, McCulloch, T, Daly, M and Kettle, M (2022) *Newly qualified social workers in Scotland: A five-year longitudinal study final report* [online] https://www.sssc.uk.com/publications/downloads/2025/04/Newly-qualified-social-workers-in-Scotland-a-five-year-longitudinal-study.pdf.

Green, M (2020) *Neurodiversity: What is it and what does it look like across races* [online] https://www.open.edu/openlearn/health-sports-psychology/mental-health/neurodiversity-what-it-and-what-does-it-look-across-races.

Guthrie and Solomon (2024) *Neurodiversity in the social work profession* [online] https://www.researchinpractice.org.uk/all/news-views/2024/march/neurodiversity-in-the-social-work-profession.

Hawkey, D and Borkowski, T (2003) *Working styles questionnaire, British psychological society* [online] https://explore.bps.org.uk/content/test-review/bpstest.2003.wsq, https://doi.org/10.53841/bpstest.2003.wsq.

Helm, D and Roesch-Marsh, A (2017) 'The ecology of judgement: A model for understanding and improving social work judgements', *British Journal of Social Work*, 47(5): 1361–1376, https://doi.org/10.1093/bjsw/bcw091.

Helm, D (2022) 'Theorising social work sense-making: Developing a model of peer-aided judgement and decision making', *British Journal of Social Work*, 52(4): 2329–2347, https://doi.org/10.1093/bjsw/bcab178.

Hochschild, AR (1983) *The managed heart commercialization of human feeling*. University of California Press, Berkeley.

Honey, P and Mumford, A (2006) *The learning styles questionnaire: 80 item version*, Peter Honey Publications, Maidenhead.

Kinman, G and Grant, L (2020) 'Emotional demands, compassion and mental health in social workers', *Occupational Medicine*, 70(2): 89–94, https://doi:10.1093/occmed/kqz144.

Knowles, MS (1984) *Andragogy in action. Applying modern principles of adult education*, Jossey Bass, San Francisco.

Kolb, DA (1984) *Experiential learning: Experience as the source of learning and development*, Prentice Hall, Englewood Cliffs.

Maclean, S, Finch, J and Tedam, P (2018) *SHARE: A new model for social work*, Kirwin Maclean Associates Ltd, Staffordshire.

van Manen, M (2014) *Phenomenology of practice*, Routledge, London.

McCulloch, T, Grant, S, Daly, M, Sen, R and Ferguson, G (2024) 'Embedding learning as a practice of value: Learning from the experiences of early career social workers in Scotland', *The British Journal of Social Work*, 54(7): 2977–2995, https://doi.org/10.1093/bjsw/bcae072.

Newton, PM (2015) 'The learning styles myth is thriving in higher education', *Frontiers in Psychology*, 6: 1908, https://doi.org/10.3389/fpsyg.2015.01908.

Open University (2024) *Practice educator refresher module*, The Open University, Milton Keynes.

Rai, L, Ferguson, G and Giddings, L (2025) 'Writing as social work: Thematic review of the literature', *The British Journal of Social Work*, 55(1): 25–44, https://doi.org/10.1093/bjsw/bcae124.

Rose, S, McCusker, P, Mitchell, M, Roesch-Marsh, A, Jian, M and Petrova, L (2025) 'Self-care in social work: An imperative or beyond reach?', *The British Journal of Social Work*, 55(3): 1455–1473, https://doi.org/10.1093/bjsw/bcae204.

Scottish Government, NHS Education for Scotland, COSLA, Resilience Learning Partnership and Improvement Service (2023) *A roadmap for creating trauma-informed and responsive change: Guidance for organisations, systems and workforces in Scotland* [online] https://www.traumatransformation.scot/implementation/.

SSSC (2019) *Standards in social work education*, Scottish Social Services Council, Dundee [online] https://learn.sssc.uk.com/siswe/siswe.html.

SSSC (2024) *NQSW supported year overview and guidance 2024* [online] https://www.nqsw.sssc.uk.com/resource/nqsw-supported-year-overview-and-guidance/.

Tedam, P (2013) 'The MANDELA model of practice learning', *The Journal of Practice Teaching and Learning*, 11(2): 60–76, https://doi.org/10.1921/jpts.v11i2.264.

Thompson, N (2017) *Theorizing practice*, Second edition, Palgrave Macmillan, London.

Thompson, S and Thompson, N (2023) *The critically reflective practitioner*, Bloomsbury, London.

Thompson, A, Harvey, A and Norris, M (2024) 'Managing reasonable adjustments', Chapter 14 in Wareing, MP (ed) *Practice supervision and assessment in nursing, health and social care*, Routledge, Abingdon, pp. 178–193.

Vallely, J (2020) *Navigating Evidence: A tool to support evidence use in practice* IRISS, Glasgow [online] https://www.iriss.org.uk/resources/tools/navigating-evidence.

Webb, S (2016) *Professional identity and social work: The Routledge Companion on the professions and professionalism*, Routledge, London.

Wiles, F and Vicary, S (2019) 'Picturing social work, puzzles and passion: Exploring and developing transnational professional identities', *Social Work Education*, 38(1): 47–62, https://doi.org/10.1080/02615479.2018.1553236.

Chapter 5

Practice learning as a social work student in Scotland

Introduction

This chapter helps social work students think about how to maximise learning in practice placements to develop their knowledge and skills. This includes exploring strategies for learning while being assessed against the Standards in Social Work Education (SiSWE) in Scotland (SSSC, 2019). The ethos of these requirements is summarised and demystified for students and practice educators. The importance of engaging in reflective professional supervision is also considered. Different aspects of the practice learning process are highlighted, and the importance of these experiences in setting foundations for a social work career is established.

Chapter aims

By the end of the chapter, you will be able to:

- understand the Scottish requirements for practice learning;
- describe the SiSWE and Ethical Principles;
- plan your personal strategy to maximise practice learning opportunities.

Practice learning for social work students in Scotland

Practice learning forms a major, mandatory part of qualifying social work education in Scotland as outlined in Chapter 1 with the importance of learning in direct practice the subject of Chapter 2. The International Federation of Social Workers (IFSW) also highlight the centrality of practice learning in their global standards, stating that it 'must be sufficient in duration and complexity of tasks and learning opportunities to ensure that students are prepared for professional practice' (IFSW, 2020, p15). The significance of practice learning for social workers is 'felt (and appreciated) long after the point of qualification…just how much placements mattered to participants: their effects and lasting impact on professional development' (Grant et al., 2022, p9). Social workers reflecting on their learning across the career identify the significance of their qualifying placements (Ferguson, 2021: Grant et al., 2022). The placement setting has often influenced the employment choices that social workers subsequently made. Pre-qualifying nursing placement experiences also suggest that these are influential in career pathways (Wareing et al., 2018).

DOI: 10.4324/9781041057598-8

Scottish requirements

In Scotland, students must have completed 180 days in directly supervised practice learning in a service delivery setting, assessed by a Practice Educator who is a qualified social worker from September 2027 (SSSC, 2024b). Although programmes might seem different across the nation as configurations in the arrangements will be decided by each university, the requirements are set out in the forthcoming revised Framework for Social Work Education in Scotland. Universities will have clear guidance and protocols for arranging, managing and monitoring their practice learning opportunities as part of their Scottish Social Services Council (SSSC) approval to deliver social work qualifications. They 'must ensure that all students have the practice learning opportunities they need to demonstrate that they meet the SiSWE' (SSSC, 2024b).

Within the overall requirements, practice learning must include 'experience of statutory social work functions and tasks involving legal interventions, including but not limited to the protection of children and vulnerable adults ideally in a local authority setting' (SSSC, 2024b). Additional requirements that practice learning opportunities 'must offer contrast both between placements and between the placement and the students usual place of work' (SSSC, 2024b) are also included. It is therefore a complex endeavour for universities to manage the logistics of placement matching against the available opportunities in their area. Students have always qualified via a wonderfully diverse range of services across the country.

Learning in practice

Massive decisions – you're not making them on your own but you are part of the system that is making these huge decisions about how people's lives are going. I think that responsibility, that is a huge kind of learning curve when you're becoming a social worker it's fine to talk about that kind of thing in the classroom but to be actually going out and doing that. When you are becoming a social worker, you can read as much as you want but until it becomes actually the point where you're having to do these things – and I think for me it was something as massive as telling a child they are away to move and doing all the practicalities and the emotions of doing that.

(Sylvia in Ferguson, 2021, p120)

Supporting your practice learning

Although students will be placed in a wide range of service delivery settings, the standards that they are assessed against are the same. Universities will also provide considerable details to students about how the specific arrangements for their practice learning will be integrated into their degree programme, along with documentation to support every stage, so this is always important to heed. A team of people might support social workers at this stage:

- university staff who arrange placements and relevant tutors;
- agency/service staff who coordinate arrangements in organisations;

- a designated link worker to support daily practice and manage work tasks;
- a practice educator who will formally supervise and assess students;
- other workers in the team or organisation.

The roles of people involved will be laid out in university documentation and form an important part of negotiating how things will work for you in your learning agreement that is developed at the start of a practice learning period. The people who arrange placements in services will most usually have many other roles, and in some organisations, there may not be anyone who formally holds this responsibility. There will however always be a designated contact between the organisation and the university, even if this is the link worker or practice educator themselves. The practice educator will be either on-site within the practice organisation, in which case you may not also have a link worker, or off-site where they will undertake this role as an external independent. In Scotland, the requirements are in a transition period that will expect that 'the Practice Educator must be a registered Social Worker who also holds a relevant Practice Teaching qualification' (SSSC, 2024b). These requirements which (from 2027) mean that your practice educator will be competent in the profession that they are assessing and understand how to support learning in a social services context. You should be able to see a profile for the agency and practice educator when you are matched to a placement, and you 'must have a different practice educator for each period of assessed practice learning' (SSSC, 2024b).

The SiSWE in Scotland

The SiSWE cover the knowledge, skills and demonstrated competence that all students are assessed against. These standards are underpinned by six Ethical Principles that are integral to what is expected of all students, and these extend to newly qualified social workers. The SiSWE, Ethical Principles and SSSC Codes of Practice for Social Service Workers (SSSC, 2024a) all come together in students' practice learning evidence as summarised in Table 5.1.

While Table 5.1 provides a summary, full details form an important part of what students will explore and annotate in written analytical work and practice educators will use to assess. When the revised SiSWE were published by the SSSC in 2019, a comprehensive web space was created to host the details and provide students, educators and organisations with resources to support learning which are highly recommended. The SiSWE themselves are broken down into a series of elements which provide crucial details of what knowledge, skills and demonstrated competence are expected; there are three columns which help explain these.

If students are asked about the SiSWE, they commonly associate these with providing evidence and of being assessed. The SiSWE cover both academic and practice elements of social work programmes, but often students become aware of them when they enter the assessed practice stages.

Reflective questions

- What ways do the standards relate to your practice learning setting?
- What standards seem most important to you as a student or practice educator?
- What might be the benefits of the SiSWE to those who are receiving a social work service?

Table 5.1 The SiSWE, Ethical Principles and SSSC Codes of Practice for Social Service Workers

Ethical Principles

Social justice and equality; Respecting diversity; Human rights and dignity; Self-determination; Partnership, participation and co-production; Honesty and integrity

Standards in Social Work Education

Standard 1. Prepare for practice and work in partnership with individuals, children, parents, families and extended families, carers, groups and communities, professionals and organisations.

Standard 2. Plan, undertake, review and evaluate social work practice with individuals, children, parents, families and extended families, carers, groups, communities and other professionals.

Standard 3. Assess and manage risk to individuals, children, parents, families and extended families, carers, groups, communities, self and colleagues.

Standard 4. Demonstrate professional confidence and competence in social work practice.

Standard 5. Manage and be accountable, with supervision and support, for own social work practice within the organisation.

Standard 6. Work in partnership with individuals, children, parents, families and extended families, carers, groups and communities to address and manage their needs, views and circumstances.

Codes of Practice for Social Service Workers

1 I must protect and promote the rights and interests of individuals and carers.
2 I must build and maintain the trust and confidence of individuals and carers.
3 I must promote the wellbeing and independence of individuals and carers while protecting them, as far as possible, from harm.
4 I must recognise that individuals have the right to take risks and will work with them to understand and manage those risks.
5 I must be accountable for the quality of my work and take responsibility for maintaining and improving my knowledge and skills.
6 I must uphold public trust and confidence.

Students can be apprehensive about the SiSWE and remain unsure about what they really mean. It can be very helpful to discuss how the SiSWE come to life in your practice from an early stage. It is important that they are not fragmented as they connect in your practice, so thinking about the work that you are doing and the people you are working with is the best place to start. You can then recognise the knowledge and skills that you are using, or that you need to develop more fully as you progress. The standards can be helpful in articulating what social work is all about, including working in partnership with people and challenging oppression.

A closer exploration of the SiSWE

In Standard 1, which has three parts, the focus is on preparation for social work contact, involvement, effective engagement with people who use social work services and assessing needs. The social context of peoples' lives, diversity, inequality and the impact of disadvantage are strongly highlighted in Standard 1 detail. While the title of the standard seems straightforward, these themes of social justice are woven throughout the Standards and Ethical Principles and were strengthened in the 2019 revision to make them prominent. Standard 2 has seven parts and covers a wide range of knowledge and skills relating to planning, intervening and reviewing practice with 'individuals, children, parents, families and extended families, carers, groups, communities and other professionals' (SSSC, 2019). Understanding the cultural context of practice and the impact of discrimination remains strong across all six standards. When revised in 2019 the importance of 'prevention and early intervention' (2.1) was strengthened along with developing 'effective networks' (2.5). Working in an interprofessional context is also as a strong theme in Standard 5. It is important to explore the details in Standard 2 and think about how practice is likely to cover the range. It is also helpful to see how the standards all come together.

Standard 3 acknowledges the skills and knowledge that social workers need across the age span and continuum of wellbeing and protection work. This includes awareness of risk to self and colleagues as well as the work you are doing with people in services. Although these issues are very explicit in Standard 3, they are woven through the other standards too in recognition that this is a crucial aspect of the social work role. For example, knowledge and skills relating to risk are explicit in 2.2 and 2.7. Standards 4 and 5 underpin everything else in the SiSWE because they cover so much about how you engage as a social work student, use knowledge to inform practice, develop your professional approach and demonstrate commitment to learning. Taking charge of your learning and making it meaningful for you is helpful whatever stage you are at (SSSC, 2024a, p5). It is impossible to meet the other standards without 4 and 5 being clearly evidenced. Understanding what you are doing and why you are doing it remains important across the career so use of different types of evidence to inform your practice is essential. SSSC (2024b) highlight that you 'must demonstrate the ability to use critical reflection and link theory to practice in both placements'.

While this chapter has not focussed on critical reflection specifically, this must be noted as such a fundamental part of social work learning and practice at all stages. Also fundamental to all social work practice is the importance of engagement with and learning from people who are using the service that you are placed in (see Chapter 9). Self-awareness and management of self is also central (see Chapter 4). Standard 6 is often thought about last and is sometimes skimmed over as it has only one part: 'Work in partnership with people receiving services, carers and communities to achieve greater independence and direct or maintain their own support, demonstrating social work values and ethical practice'. There are very important elements that are explicit in the detail about the responsibility of social work students to understand the 'different needs faced by people' and 'the impact and inter relationship of disadvantage and social divisions arising from factors such as: social class; gender; disability; culture; race; migration; asylum status' (SSSC, 2019, 6.1). Understanding and 'upholding the law in respect of discrimination', 'responding to prejudice, institutional discrimination and structural inequality' and managing 'own and others' prejudices and value conflicts' are also clear (SSSC, 2019, 6.1). This is one example of how the SiSWE integrate fundamental responsibilities for social workers as statutory agents in using this power to take an empowering, anti-oppressive and rights-based approach. Practice learning should also model inclusivity and anti-oppressive approaches by all those involved in supporting placements.

Reflective questions

- What do you think are the most important aspects of a practice learning placement?
- In which aspects might there be tensions for you or others?
- How can you retain a focus on your specific learning needs?

Where your practice learning happens

Practice learning is 'based in a service delivery setting in the statutory, private or voluntary sector' and 'the setting must provide the learning opportunities necessary for the student to meet The Standards in Social Work Education' (SSSC, 2024b). Wondering where you will be placed is often a source of apprehension for students in terms of the geographic location but also the service setting and focus. Social work students like many other professionals in training are managing competing demands balancing work, family or caring responsibilities with study. Practice learning requires full-time attendance on-site, and therefore, this can add to the pressure that social work students experience or anticipate.

Ferguson and Sicat (2024) remind us that social work programmes need to equip students for working in a statutory context (whether or not the individual eventually does), recently strengthened in Scottish requirements (SSSC, 2024b). While there is significant debate about the nature and definition of what constitutes appropriate experience and the availability of statutory placements (e.g., Samuel, 2024), this is concerned with developing students' capacity to understand and undertake statutory tasks associated with legal requirements, assessment and decision-making in care and protection, justice or mental health practice. Sicat and Ferguson also highlight that the distinction between settings is not as clear as it initially sounds with third sector services often commissioned to provide services on behalf of local authorities blurring what counts as statutory. In many local areas, there are arrangements for working across settings to maximise learning opportunities.

There is also substantial evidence of many exceptional quality third sector practice learning opportunities (IRISS, 2025). Some studies have found that there may be implications of the cultural context of the work setting and whether 'understanding of professional identity and the discreteness of the social work role' are developed 'in settings which do not require specific social work skills or where they are managed by other professions' (Grant et al., 2022, p114). This means that it is important for students in all settings, irrespective of where they might choose to practice in the future, to be able to focus on understanding professional authority and accountability in social work roles commensurate with the protected title of Social Worker. Enhancement and development of quality practice learning opportunities across the sector remains at the fore of the social work education agenda across all partners.

Learning in practice

At very short notice I was asked to just come and be with her and one of the workers there made play dough and I sat with that girl for about two hours just passing the play dough between us. It was quite calming for both of us actually and it didn't need to be much. I suppose one of the dilemmas of being a social worker is that you are working within a framework, if you're in a statutory sector where it's about rules, assessment, it's about quite formal processes, it's often about conflict as well and sometimes those rules and the presenting problems and issues and challenges and all that kind of stuff draw you away from the person. I felt that in that place you know it wasn't just mechanical, it was total dialogue if you like, she couldn't speak you know but there was just you know a sort of interaction, a live interaction that was important and one of my views of social work in every context is that it's about good communication, it's about dialogue, it's about not losing the person no matter what formal process you are engaged in.

(Reuben in Ferguson, 2021, p89)

The practice learning and assessment process

Universities will provide detailed guidance about preparation and agreements for practice learning which is always your main point of reference. There is a sequence of stages in practice learning opportunities and important things to be thinking about (and doing) at each:

- identifying any support or practical arrangements that will enable you to learn;
- developing your professional identity and network;
- gathering and using feedback to support your learning;
- preparing for and using professional supervision to support practice;
- reflecting on practice, thinking about ethics, self-awareness and self-care;
- being proactive, planning for and taking responsibility for your learning.

At all stages, you should be thinking about how to maximise your profile and how you present yourself as an emerging social work professional. This means thinking about what to include in any written and verbal communication with agency representatives, your practice educator and link supervisor or team. This is a key part of developing a career-long professional network of peers and allies.

Being assessed

It is important that all students are clear about how they will be assessed in practice learning and a range of evidence will be drawn together by the practice educator to inform their recommendation about whether you meet the SiSWE. In most cases, the following evidence is used to inform assessment in practice learning:

- your direct practice;
- feedback from people who use the service;
- reflective discussion and written accounts;
- agency records and reports;
- engagement in the professional supervision process;
- informal and formal observation;
- feedback from colleagues and link workers;
- any specific university requirements.

It is essential that assessment is clear, robust and fair, a core part of all practice educator training. Assessment is a process throughout each period of practice learning, and students should receive regular feedback on their progress towards the standards and have a clear plan at all stages. There will usually be a formal mid-point stage where practice educators will indicate the progress as to whether the student is on track for a pass recommendation or otherwise, and in both cases to identify the focus for the remainder of the placement. At the end of the practice learning period, there will be a formal report provided by the practice educator taking all of the evidence into account and detailing whether the SiSWE have been met. While students are observed informally in the course of their practice, there are formal observations that are a central component of the process, and each 'period of practice learning should include a minimum of three observations of direct practice, two of which must be conducted by the allocated Practice Educator' (SSSC, 2024b). Further to this, 'the third must be conducted by someone approved by the allocated practice educator but who is not necessarily a qualified practice educator themselves' (SSSC, 2024b) and a 'minimum of two observations of practice must involve direct work with people using the service' (SSSC, 2024b). Planning well for observations is important, and universities will use appropriate documentation to record these.

There is a high expectation on university providers of qualifying education to ensure readiness of social workers to practice and equip them for the newly qualified and early career transition stages (Grant *et al.*, 2016). While there has been a requirement for a transitionary individual learning plan since the 2003 Framework, recent developments have foregrounded this, embedding the requirement firmly. This means that planning for learning can be seen as a continuing process throughout practice learning at the student stage, the Newly Qualified Social Worker (NQSW) Supported Year and subsequent career.

Reflective questions

- What ways can you track your progress in meeting the SiSWE in practice learning?
- How can you ask for and use meaningful feedback to help your learning from people who you are working with?
- Make a few notes and identify any actions to help plan your practice learning.

Summary points

- All social work students in Scotland have the same overall requirements and are assessed against the SiSWE and Ethical Principles.
- Practice learning settings are diverse but must provide the learning opportunities necessary for the student to meet the SiSWE.
- The SiSWE contain important details and can help students articulate their social work practice.
- Students can take responsibility to maximise their learning in practice through planning and engaging in supervision.

Further reading

A quick read

The SSSC dedicated Standards in Social Work Education (SiSWE) website provides an absolute treasure trove of resources to support development of essential skills, knowledge and values. There are a broad range of materials including those that help support reflection and supervision. There are a great range of resources for students and educators (SSSC, 2019).

A helpful model

Collingwood's Theory Cycle remains a firm favourite for students and practice educators drawing together values and theories for informing and intervening. Developed in Scotland, its reach has since extended across many nations as a creative and practical way to hold a person at the centre of practice analysis (Collingwood *et al.*, 2007).

A deeper dive

Sue and Neil Thompson's book, *The Critically Reflective Practitioner*, provides an easy-to-use resource for any stage of the social work career. With clear explanations of theories about learning and reflection, the book is rooted in Sue and Neil's expertise in the field (Thompson and Thompson, 2023).

Please also see the resources section in the Appendix.

References

Collingwood, P, Emond, R and Woodward, R (2007) 'The theory circle: A tool for learning and for practice', *Social Work Education*, 27(1): 70–83.

Ferguson, G (2021) '"When David Bowie created Ziggy Stardust" the lived experiences of social workers learning through work', Doctor of Education (EdD) Thesis, The Open University, https://doi.org/10.21954/ou.ro.0001306a.

Ferguson, G and Sicat, S (2024) 'Practice education in social work', in Wareing, MP (ed) *Practice supervision and assessment in nursing, health and social care,* Routledge, Abingdon pp.116–126.

Grant, S, Sheridan, L and Webb, S (2016) 'Newly qualified social workers' readiness for practice in Scotland', *British Journal of Social Work*, 47(2): 487–506, https://doi.org/10.1093/bjsw/bcv146.

Grant, S, McCulloch, T, Daly, M and Kettle, M (2022) *Newly qualified social workers in Scotland: A five-year longitudinal study final report* [online] https://www.sssc.uk.com/publications/downloads/2025/04/2019-Newly-qualified-social-workers-in-Scotland-A-five-year-longitudinal-study.pdf.

IFSW (2020) *Global standards for social work education and training* [online] https://www.ifsw.org/global-standards-for-social-work-education-and-training.

IRISS (2025) *Student placements in third sector organisations* [online] https://www.iriss.org.uk/resources/tools/student-placements-third-sector-organisations#:~:text=Developed%20in%20collaboration%20with%20both,and%20the%20students%20experiencing%20them.

Samuel, M (2024) *Non-statutory placements make up over half of provision for students in Scotland, Community Care* [online] https://www.communitycare.co.uk/2024/03/15/non-statutory-placements-make-up-over-half-of-provision-for-students-in-scotland-report-reveals/.

SSSC (2019) *Standards in social work education* [online] https://learn.sssc.uk.com/siswe/siswe.html.

SSSC (2024a) *The SSSC codes of practice* [online] https://www.sssc.uk.com/the-scottish-social-services-council/sssc-codes-of-practice/.

SSSC (2024b) *Revised standards for teaching, learning and assessment,* Scottish Social Services Council, Dundee.

Thompson, S and Thompson, N (2023) *The critically reflective practitioner*, Bloomsbury, London.

Wareing, M, Taylor, R, Wilson, A and Sharples, A (2018) 'Impact of clinical placements on graduates' choice of first staff-nurse post', *British Journal of Nursing*, 27(20): 1180–1185, https://doi.org/10.12968/bjon.2018.27.20.1180.

Chapter 6

Learning in diverse social work practice settings to do an extraordinary job

Introduction

This chapter explores the extraordinary diverse range of places in which social workers learn including in statutory, third sector and private services. The workplace is recognised as a primary site for learning across the career, and messages from research are explored about navigating landscape and places. The generic requirements of social work education are considered alongside strengthening the confidence of students and practice educators in recognising transferable learning irrespective of the setting. This chapter highlights the richness of learning in grassroots activist organisations, specialist services as well as core local authority and health partnerships working with children and adults. It provides a baseline for acknowledging the importance of understanding workplaces and workplace learning theory for practice learning. Social work is a profession like no other, and learning as a social worker has multiple complex layers. Examples from research are drawn on where social workers describe learning through their direct practice and how they learn through navigating their work tasks.

Chapter aims

By the end of the chapter, you will be able to:

- describe Scottish social work practice settings for learning;
- understand how social workers learn within diverse practice settings;
- identify the important aspects of landscapes for learning.

The Scottish context

Learning in social work is not a simple process and involves

> the development of skills and competences which enable practitioners to undertake a role which is rooted in human rights and social justice, where ethical practice needs to be negotiated within a work role where there are competing moral, legal, organisational and policy demands.
>
> (Ferguson, 2021, p11)

DOI: 10.4324/9781041057598-9

Further to this, to practice social work in Scotland needs an understanding of the Scottish context. This might sound simple, but social work policy, practice and regulation are very different across the four nations of the United Kingdom (UK) and international contexts even though the International Federation of Social Workers (IFSW) Global definition (IFSW, 2014) may be shared.

In Wales, there is a powerful emphasis on embedding the *Welsh way* in social work education and practice which integrates an appreciation of the culture, languages, principles of policy and specific legislation (Livingston *et al.*, 2023). Students are required to demonstrate their ability to analyse their practice with explicit connection to the Welsh context. So, for Scotland, it ought to be a similar priority that we are clear in supporting students, qualified workers and our partner organisations to recognise what is unique to the Scottish context and, of course, the multiple diverse communities therein.

Reflective questions

- How is Scottish social work different to other countries?
- Why might it be important to understand the Scottish context?
- What are the nuances of social work practice in settings that you are familiar with?

These may have been difficult questions to answer, however you may have immediately thought about the different legislation that applies in Scotland. You might also have thought about the way in which social work in Scotland is involved in justice practice or the specific and unique Children's Hearing System. Alternatively, you might have thought about the geography of Scotland, rural or island contexts for practice. Scottish social work is continually evolving, and understanding how it shapes within the political arena remains important.

In the past few years, practice in Scotland has been driven by the incorporation of the United Nations Convention on the Rights of the Child (UNCRC) into legislation in 2024; the rise of The Promise (The Promise Scotland, 2025), a shared commitment to care experienced children that they grow up loved, safe and respected; a continued focus on Self-Directed Support (Social Work Scotland, 2024); and an overarching approach to becoming trauma-informed and responsive (Scottish Government *et al.*, 2023). These are just some dominant forces shaping practice expectations that have individual peoples' experiences and interests at the centre and which are likely to feature in social workers' training and continuing professional learning.

While this book does not intend to cover all details of Scottish practice, this chapter focuses on some important issues for learning in this landscape. Ideas from social workers' experiences of learning in diverse practice settings will be used to highlight how and what they learn. There are helpful summaries of pressing issues in relation to the Scottish context, for example, caseload demands (Miller and Barrie, 2022), the rural context (Turbett, 2019a) and the legal and policy context (e.g., Turbett, 2019b). The final section of this book takes a tour around Scotland, signposts to different resources, places and spaces that have inspired social workers' learning and details sources of continuing professional learning.

Learning in social work practice in Scotland

The web model (Figure 2.1) includes navigating tasks, landscape and places as distinct important themes. Learning in the workplace must combine an understanding of the nature of the work and place in which it happens. Social work is often categorised across three main practice areas in Scotland: social work with children and families, social work with adults and social work in justice settings. Services are located within local authorities, third sector organisations, integrated health partnerships and some private organisations. Social workers are qualified with a generic qualification and when registered can work in any of these areas. There are multiple specific aspects of practice and specialist services within and across these areas, and many social workers operate in organisations or settings which may not easily be categorised so simply.

Social work practice across settings is concerned with holistic, social-ecological and strengths-based perspectives informing wide-ranging skills to assess and intervene. Social workers are involved in work that includes completing complex and comprehensive assessments and provision of reports to assist decision-making and to make legal applications. They are also involved in contributing to multi-agency practice to support children, young people or adults and planning with people ensuring that they are fully involved in decision-making about their care. Social workers are also directly involved in providing therapeutic interventions and have a significant history of doing so, albeit the opportunities all depend on roles and settings.

Reflective questions

- Identify the specific focus of any social work settings or services that you are familiar with.
- How would you describe the evidence base and legislation that characterises practice?
- What ways can social workers learn the required knowledge and skills in this setting?

While there is no doubt that the specialist skills and knowledge for different settings are often clear, it can be harder to identify the core, generic ones which can be continually developed as a professional social worker.

Social work with children and families

This is a diverse area of practice across statutory and third sector settings, fundamentally centred on the wellbeing, support and protection of children and young people, from pre-birth across ages depending on the role, promoting and upholding their rights. Social work with children and families might include therapeutic/support work; comprehensive assessments, including of risk; child protection; work with parents, including assessment of parenting capacity; adoption and fostering practice and specialist interventions. The Getting It Right for Every Child (GIRFEC) policy and associated National Practice Model remain at the centre of social work practice with children and families (Scottish Government, 2022a). A report linked to consultation on development of a National Care Service provides an overview of social services provided to children and families in Scotland (Scottish Government, 2022b), which includes data on reason for social work involvement.

Social work with adults

A diverse area of practice across statutory and third sector settings, fundamentally centred on the wellbeing, support and protection of adults, from the age of 16 across the lifespan depending on the role, promoting and upholding their rights. Social work with adults might include practice with older people, dementia, frailty, palliative and end-of-life care; mental health, drugs and alcohol, learning disabilities, physical and sensory disabilities and autism; support to carers and other specialist services.

Social work in justice settings

Social work in justice settings has a key role and long tradition in Scottish social work including work in court, prisons and the community which aims to reduce reoffending, increase social inclusion and rehabilitation and help protect the public from serious harm. Social work is a key partner with significant expertise in multi-agency public protection arrangements. Practice in this area might include working with people with a wide range of multiple and often complex issues affecting them, such as domestic abuse, sexual offending, hate crime and extremism, violence, substance use and mental health. Full information and excellent learning materials can be found via Community Justice Scotland and the Scottish Governments' dedicated information on justice social work. Social workers in justice settings may be involved in comprehensive assessments; supporting people on court-directed orders; provision of evidence-informed therapeutic and behaviour change individual and groupwork interventions. Specific practice in youth justice is also an important area in Scotland with many excellent learning resources available in the Children and Young People's Centre for Justice (CYCJ) including on the child's journey (CYCJ, 2021).

These basic descriptors do not, of course, go anywhere near to covering the breadth and scope of practice but are included for readers less familiar with the Scottish context. In all settings, social work contributes expertise to adult social care and support services across multiple formal and informal partnerships in local areas as well as delivery of specialist practice areas. Every area of practice has a strong evidence base with creative, widely used research summaries, toolkits and guidance produced by Iriss very popular for social workers' learning. The SSSC developed an excellent summary of key legislation and policy to guide social workers returning to practice during the COVID-19 pandemic which remains a helpful summary collection (SSSC, 2020).

Student practice learning placements

Student placements take place in all these settings, and discussion often centres around whether a setting is statutory or otherwise. This is not a dualistic debate. It is essential to understand and develop capability to undertake the type of statutory tasks which can be carried out by people holding the protected title of Social Worker as part of initial and continuing professional learning irrespective of setting. There are over 45,000 third sector services in Scotland (Scottish Council for Voluntary Organisations (SCVO)), many of which are focused on supporting people, social care and promoting equality. There are many high-quality providers and those where some services are directly commissioned by local authorities to meet their statutory obligations. Third sector services often have their origin in collective action rooted in the voices of people's experiences and longstanding delivery of outcomes-focused practice in authentic co-produced services. Integrated health partnerships are also central to the delivery of social work services in Scotland and need considered in relation to professional social work. Any learning setting needs to understand the needs of learners within them including the Standards for Social Work Education and the requirements of the Newly Qualified Social Worker Supported Year. Careful negotiation and planning are essential for any social work placement, ensuring that the right conditions and expertise can support students.

Navigating complex landscapes and places of work

The idea of learning in landscapes of practice (Wenger-Traynor and Wenger-Traynor, 2015) suggests that landscapes are formed of the community and shared knowledge of professional groups. Places and spaces formed essential elements of social workers' learning and are fundamentally connected to their embodied experiences and how they navigate workplace tasks (Ferguson, 2021). Places of work within these landscapes are a primary site for learning (Billett, 2001), and research with social workers reveals that they are often working in spaces that are physically or psychologically isolated. There is no route map and no overall guidebook to navigate these workplaces, and the physical landscape can change as services and roles change. Social workers also describe navigating the practice landscape with an internal ethical compass, guiding them to work out what to do or how to find their way (Ferguson, 2021).

Workplaces

Social work happens in courts, hospital wards, community venues, *'up dark roads, in the middle of the countryside, in the dark, to get a sheriff to sign this CPO* [Child Protection Order]' (Maisie in Ferguson, 2021, p97). The home visit is also one of the most common places for social workers to be working. Ferguson's (2009) research demonstrates the complexity of the home visit as a workplace that involves managing the boundaries of space, expectations of role and the immediacy of uncertainty. Social workers describe learning through the many metaphors such as the setting of court as theatre learning lines and working out the part (Ferguson, 2021). It is essential that we understand the workplace is a very complex arena for social work practice.

Learning in practice

The building itself was really risky, I arrived and got told there's your room and it was right beside the front door and I remember sitting at the desk writing and turning round and a massive big dog right behind my arm, came wandering in and its owner then subsequently came wandering in, affected by substances so, it was winter, it was dark, it's on the ground floor, but the window let no light in and they got fed up replacing the glass they had put this sort of Perspex you couldn't see out, so there was no natural light… I just felt it was an assault on all the senses.

(Kathleen in Ferguson, 2021, p113)

What else makes up the landscape and places of practice?

Social workers described their learning as encountering different worlds, sometimes a familiar space and at other times a culture shock (Ferguson, 2021). Metaphors for learning in practice were used by social workers to elaborate on how they navigated the workplace. Battle metaphors were used to explain how social workers learned about 'being on the side-lines' (Caroline), 'trying to get over the threshold' (Sophie), 'like a minefield' (Makine) and 'reflecting from a place of safety' (Carol) in Ferguson (2021 p146). Makine also described an example of being in an office where 'the world is on fire' to represent the heightened emotional and physical experience of learning in crisis work (Ferguson, 2021, p167).

Other elements of the working landscape for social workers include the social and economic context of people's lives, including poverty, neglect, substance use and complex family dynamics (Ferguson, 2021). These aspects of place are part of social workers' experiences of learning through work. The landscape was also seen by social workers to be characterised by the influences of legislation and policy which shaped how things were done, what became priority and the nature of working environments. Organisational culture and the position of the social worker within this are also hugely influential in opportunities to learn (see Chapter 8). As workplaces continue to change shape in relation to agile working and integration of services, social workers may have limited direct contact with one another. This has many implications for learning in that other social workers are essential to the learning of their peers (see Chapter 9). Within these workplace settings, many different professionals are learning in integrated partnerships or multidisciplinary teams. Within this partnership context, it is essential to understand the specific needs and nuances of each profession for learning to be effective and for shared knowledge to generate.

Navigating tasks

Within the landscape, social workers are also making sense of the work that they do. Social work as a profession faces ambiguity of role, task and the ambivalence of the public (Moriarty et al., 2015). Social workers describe the immediacy of this within practice, undertaking tasks that were indescribable and sometimes conflicting or contradictory with different skills required for different settings (Ferguson, 2021). Social work tasks are renowned for their complexity (Hood, 2015). This context makes learning as a social worker complicated; if it is difficult to define the social work role and task, it is impossible to define the knowledge and skills that need to be learned. This is therefore a challenge for social work educators. Within work tasks, social workers experience significant learning through participative processes such as observation, experience, imitation or transmission (Eraut, 2009), all of which could take place within a single event.

Learning in practice

I used to say to people, it'd be really good to be something like a joiner or plumber or something, that people look at your work and go 'that's a really good job you've done there', and they can see it. In social work, it's seldom, it's never as clear cut as that is it?

(Karl in Ferguson, 2021, p130)

Social work is 'not a normal job' (Maisie in Ferguson, 2021, p96). Very difficult tasks can feel like they become the ordinary work of the profession, but these remain extraordinary. Learning about the enormity of decisions and the impact on families are central to social workers' professional learning: 'the importance of understanding the unique lives of people, keeping children alive and safe, trying to reduce chaos, trying to be realistic and understanding risk' (Ferguson, 2021, p149). Social workers often share learning where this has related to very difficult situations, for example, with a young person doused in petrol (Makine), a father who had killed the family pet (Sylvia), the birth of a baby who had died in utero (Karl) and a boy whose father had murdered their mother (Karl). Social workers also describe learning from powerful and positive scenarios all linked with the deeply personal journey of their professional development. Small parts of a practice task can also be meaningful for social workers' learning, for example, as experienced by Reuben in his interaction with a young person using play dough shown in Chapter 4. Finding a way to work within the systems and processes of social work tasks was described by Makine using the metaphor of 'the machine' (Ferguson, 2021, p131). This relates to the experience of social workers' learning to navigate the machine characterised by trying to balance ethical and moral practice within the demands of the system.

Learning in practice

I got caught up in the whole conflict between … the systems that we operate within and … engaging with the people you are working with, to have relationships, to effect change and …how those two don't necessarily marry up. … It is almost like a constant duality, just being pulled in different directions, trying to marry that tension, work out that tension between the two…it is trying to find the balance…I always just found a tension about it. I love doing the job, and I don't like doing the job, because I don't like the framework and the rest of the kind of conflict.

(Makine in Ferguson, 2021, p134)

Creating opportunities to learn

Billett (2004) proposes that workplace affordances are the aspects of the workplace that offer possibilities to learn. Billet suggests that allocation of work and how different tasks are introduced need careful orchestration to maximise learning. Social work poses a problem as there are no tasks that will be the same on more than one occasion, although there may be similarities in their type, function or product (such as an assessment report of a particular type or for a particular audience). There is also no set pattern of what work tasks will be available at any point in time within a service. This means that the distribution of work in a way that supports learning can be hard to plan. Opportunities to learn in the workplace do not usually have a clear curriculum or robust-associated pedagogy resulting in learning opportunities that are not optimised (Billett, 2004). Developing knowledgeability (Wenger-Traynor and Wenger-Traynor, 2015) defines the professional skills and competences within a landscape which are hard to articulate but are understood within it. The concept of knowledgeability may be helpful for social work to prepare for dynamic work scenarios and appreciate the nature of knowledge that is created within the profession.

While this chapter has undoubtedly represented the complexity of social work as an extraordinary job, social workers' accounts of their learning are incredible and shine a light on just what it takes. Articulating how complex learning in this field is can help convey what is involved in being a social worker. It is essential for social work to be able to articulate what it does without describing merely in relation to other professions. Chapter 7 continues to explore professional learning as a career-long endeavour that is part of professional social work.

Reflective questions

- How would you describe learning for social workers?
- What is needed to support social workers to learn in these diverse practice settings?
- Where can opportunities for social workers to learn across settings be enhanced?

Summary points

- The Scottish context of social work is important for learners and educators.
- Navigating diverse workplaces and tasks is part of social work professional learning.
- Developing professional authority and decision-making is learned through practice.
- Social work is an extraordinary job.

Further reading

A quick read

Now in its 12th edition, *Social Care and the Law in Scotland* by Siobhan Maclean and Mark Shiner is a superb and easy-to-use reference to the legal context published by Kirwin Maclean Associates. A more detailed guide to law from Andrew Farrar (*Social Work Law in Scotland*) is published by Bloomsbury.

A helpful set of resources

The *SSSC Learning Zone* (https://www.sssc.uk.com/supporting-the-workforce/learning-zone/) and the dedicated *NQSW website* (https://www.nqsw.sssc.uk.com/) are highly recommended for excellent research and evidence along with social work-specific resources to support learning.

A deeper dive

Social Work: An Introduction published by Sage, by the fantastic editors Joyce Lishman, Janine Bolger, Gary Spolander, Neil Gibson and Chris Yuill, is in its third edition and covers a wide range of knowledge, intervention and contextual information. It is a great volume which links to the Scottish Standards in Social Work Education.

Please also see the resources section in the Appendix.

References

Billett, S (2001) 'Learning through work: Workplace affordances and individual engagement', *Journal of Workplace Learning*, 13(5/6): 209–214.

Billett, S (2004) 'Workplace participatory practices: Conceptualising workplaces as learning environments', *Journal of Workplace Learning*, 16(6): 312–324.

CYCJ (2021) *The child's journey: A guide to the Scottish justice system* [online] https://content.iriss.org.uk/youthjustice/.

Eraut, M (2009) 'Transfer of knowledge between education and workplace settings', in Daniels, H, Lauder, H and Porter, J (eds) *Knowledge, values and educational policy: A critical perspective*, Taylor & Francis, United Kingdom, pp. 201–221.

Ferguson, H (2009) 'Performing child protection: Home visiting, movement and the struggle to reach the abused child', *Child and Family Social Work*, 14(4): 471–480, https://doi.org/10.1111/j.1365-2206.2009.00630.x.

Ferguson, G (2021) *When David Bowie created Ziggy Stardust: The lived experiences of social workers learning through work*, The Open University, Milton Keynes.

Hood, R (2015) 'How professionals experience complexity: An interpretative phenomenological analysis', *Child Abuse Review*, 24(2): 140–152, https://doi.org/10.1002/car.2359.

IFSW (2014) *Global definition of social work* [online] www.ifsw.org/what-is-social-work/global-definition-of-social-work/.

Livingston, W, Redcliffe, J and Quinn Aziz, A (eds) (2023) *Social work in Wales,* Policy Press, Bristol.

Miller, E and Barrie, K (2022) *Setting the bar for social work in Scotland* [online] https://socialworkscotland.org/wp-content/uploads/2022/05/Setting-the-Bar-Full-Report.pdf.

Moriarty, J, Baginsky, M and Manthorpe, J (2015) *Literature review of roles and issues within the social work profession in England* [online] https://www.professionalstandards.org.uk/docs/default-source/publications/research-paper/literature-review-roles-and-issues-within-the-social-work-profession-in-england-2015.pdf.

Scottish Government (2022a) *National practice model* [online] https://www.gov.scot/policies/girfec/national-practice-model/.

Scottish Government (2022b) *National Care Service: Social work contextual paper* [online] https://www.gov.scot/publications/national-care-service-social-work-scotland-contextual-paper/.

Scottish Government, NHS Education for Scotland, COSLA, Resilience Learning Partnership and Improvement Service (2023) *A roadmap for creating trauma-informed and responsive change: Guidance for organisations, systems and workforces in Scotland* [online] https://www.traumatransformation.scot/implementation/.

Social Work Scotland (2024) *Self-directed support* [online] https://socialworkscotland.org/sws-projects/self-directed-support/.

SSSC (2020) *Guidance to help social workers respond to COVID-19* [online] https://learn.sssc.uk.com/bitesizeguides/socialwork/.

The Promise Scotland (2025) *Focus on change strategic work programme 2025–2026* [online] https://thepromise.scot/resources/2025/strategic-workplan-2025-26.pdf.

Turbett, C (2019a) *Rural social work in Scotland* [online] https://www.iriss.org.uk/resources/insights/rural-social-work-scotland.

Turbett, C (2019b) *Social work across the UK: Legal and policy differences from a Scottish perspective* [online] https://basw.co.uk/policy-and-practice/resources/social-work-across-uk-legal-and-policy-differences-scottish.

Wenger-Trayner, E and Wenger-Traynor, B (2015) 'Learning in a landscape of practice: A framework', in Wenger-Trayner, E, Fenton-O'Creevy, M, Hutchinson, S, Kubiak, C and Wenger-Trayner, B (eds) *Learning in landscapes of practice: Boundaries, identity, and knowledgeability in practice-based learning*, Routledge, London, pp. 2–15.

Chapter 7

Continuing professional learning

Introduction

Throughout the book so far, you have been introduced to the context of learning in Scottish social work practice and many examples of how social workers learn. Continuing Professional Learning (CPL) is an integral part of professional social work across the whole of your career, in recognition of the need for up-to-date, safe and effective practice that has people's lives at the heart. This chapter outlines the importance of and opportunities for CPL as a career-long and career-wide integral aspect of social work. Learning at different stages of the career is considered, from qualifying, through early career to experienced professional. Formal and informal learning opportunities that enhance professional practice are explored aligned with social workers' deepening their knowledge and continuing to enhance their skills. Examples from social workers reveal what they have learned that is most important to them in their careers and how they learned this. By planning for what is meaningful for you, this chapter argues that professional learning is at the centre of daily social work practice beyond evolving frameworks and regulatory requirements. All the information that has been covered in previous chapters remains relevant. This chapter also discusses how those who support social workers' learning in practice settings can respond to the unique needs of this workforce group.

Chapter aims

By the end of the chapter, you will be able to:

- describe what counts as CPL in social work;
- understand the regulatory requirements for CPL;
- identify a plan for prioritising your learning.

What is CPL

Earlier chapters have explored social work as an extraordinary job that is rarely understood by people who have not been immersed in it. CPL is all about how social workers gain the necessary knowledge and skills that they need for practice throughout their career. It needs to be relevant for social workers and services and ultimately to the purpose of social work in contributing to social justice, support and protection of people. Learning includes keeping up to date with changes in legislation, policy and practice guidance but

DOI: 10.4324/9781041057598-10

also extends to deepening critical thinking, enhancing specialist skills and contributing to the professional development of other social workers. CPL is often associated with the regulatory requirements of your continued registration as a social worker with the Scottish Social Services Council (SSSC). There are specific details stipulated by the SSSC about CPL which will be discussed later in this chapter, however these need not feel restrictive; they are rooted in developing safe, effective practice.

Learning on a continuum across time and space

A continuum of CPL starts in qualifying education, through transition to newly qualified practice, building on these foundations and evolving thereafter for the whole career. It is essential that you consider your CPL in a way that is meaningful for you as the primary focus. CPL is often associated with regulatory frameworks and the expectations of employers, but tuning into what matters to you is an important reflective point for planning your learning. Social workers learn through a diverse array of informal and formal activities. The importance of learning in and through direct practice with people who are using social work services is one essential part that is critical throughout the career. Although often a focus of the early career, including the development of an Individual Learning Plan (ILP) at the transition from student to newly qualified social worker (NQSW), CPL is important at any career stage. The term career-long may be familiar to you in meaning for the whole length of time being a social worker, but the term career-wide is also helpful to describe learning that is across the scope of practice, settings and skills that are needed.

Lifelong learning has been a concept long recognised in adult education and professional learning. Barnett introduces the concept of lifewide learning which, in contrast to lifelong learning, suggests that people are 'learning in different places simultaneously... in learning spaces and ...these places may be profoundly different' (Barnett, 2011, p2). This is summarised as lifelong education happens across time, but lifewide education happens across spaces (Barnett, 2011) all relevant to the ideas discussed in the earlier chapters where places within the landscape were so relevant to social workers' learning.

What counts as CPL?

There are many informal, formal and accredited programmes and self-directed learning activities which social workers learn including:

- reflection, integrated as part of your way of being as a social worker;
- self-directed reading of journal articles, books, professional bulletins or sector guidance;
- listening to podcasts or watching film clips;
- engaging in supervision discussion and structured analysis of practice;
- peer or team discussion;
- shadowing, co-working or observation of other workers;
- traditional in-person training courses;
- undertaking online learning programmes;
- accredited qualifications in specialist practice or subjects;
- learning through everyday practice.

You may have thought about other ways that you have learned whilst reading this book.

Transitions

There are formalised processes for social workers' CPL as they work towards the end of their education in university which support transition to the NQSW Supported Year. Essential to this is developing an authentic ILP that will support you and your employer to plan and review your learning. Central to developing an authentic plan is a professional conversation about your learning with those that are supporting you, this will help articulate your learning needs and aspirations to take control of your learning as a social worker. Establishing good learning habits at the student and newly qualified stages can support effective career-long learning. At the NQSW stage, there are actually multiple transitions as social workers navigate the early career in relation to the workplace settings, sense of identity and professional learning (Grant et al., 2022). The deeply personal journey discussed in Chapter 4 is full of change and shifts in identity for social workers.

Within the social work career transitions continue as we move into new roles over time, change teams or practice focus. The concept of transitions and managing change are, of course, also central to how we understand and support people we are working with; we do not always consider what is happening for ourselves. Practice educator training programmes often consider the concepts of learning, change, resilience and growth. One of the models often used to explore the emotional journey with practice educators and students is Fisher's visual model, the Personal Transition Curve (Fisher, 2012). While this model is commonly used in relation to change in workplace settings, it is rooted in psychological theories of how people experience loss, change and growth. Fisher identifies eight stages of personal transition in response to change, ranging from 'anxiety' to 'moving forward'. As with other models, there is no expectation that the stages are linear or significant to everyone, even when experiencing the same type of change. Having a firm foundation in terms of knowledge and skills can help us prepare for the transitions that ourselves or others might experience in the social work career.

Reflective questions

- Looking back over your career what transitions can you identify?
- What kind of learning was associated with these transitions?
- How can you prepare for future changes?

You have perhaps identified personal transitions in your career stage, confidence or professional identity. In addition, or instead, you may have identified changes in practice focus or team as a key transition. It might have been difficult to pinpoint transitions, or there may have been times where there seemed to be more of an abrupt shift in your learning or career. You might not have previously thought about any learning that was associated with the changes that you have experienced as a social worker. Change often has a connection to our professional learning. New insights can lead to the shifts we experience or arise from those transitions.

Developing your craft

Social workers have often sought answers to the perpetual questions about the purpose and nature of the professional role and task (Moriarty et al., 2015; McCulloch and

Taylor, 2018). The lived experiences of social workers also reveal a sense of developing their craft as an articulation of CPL (Ferguson, 2021). Development of a craft has long been considered in the career of a tradesperson from the beginning stages, developing through experience and practice to an advanced level. Conceptions of crafting can also be considered as shaping, building, creating and developing something according to the needs or interests of the craftsperson. Using the metaphor of learning as a craft is therefore an interesting choice by the social workers signifying something under creation and development and which took time.

Learning in practice

Yes the art of practice for me, there's not a rule book you know we have all got these practice guidelines and things like that but when it comes down to the minutiae there is not a yes or a right answer for lots of things that we do sometimes if we do the same thing twice some people might say that one was right and that one wasn't right sometimes you're damned if you do and you're damned if you don't … it means a lot to me it's an incredibly privileged important job to undertake when you're going into somebody's private space … I take it very, very seriously.

(Boab in Ferguson, 2021, p79)

Characteristics of experienced and advanced social work practice beyond the early career

It has been notoriously difficult to articulate clear definitions of what social work practice at a more advanced level of this craft looks like. This is in part due to the complexity and skill that is required from the early career onwards. Social workers, managers, educators and leaders identify some of the characteristics that they regard as being part of professional learning and practice as social workers develop through their careers:

- use of professional wisdom and intuitive practice that is rooted in evidence from experience;
- in-depth critical analysis and reflection on practice examples and the impact of social work on people's lives;
- careful professional judgement, decision-making and supporting other professionals to do so;
- enhanced self-awareness, emotional intelligence, skilled use of self in practice and leadership in social work (at any level);
- authenticity, honesty and integrity in recognising own strengths, learning needs and development of solutions to address these for effective practice;
- fluency in the application of legislation and other guidance to support people, promote their rights and protect them;
- directly seeking to address inequality, discrimination and oppression fundamental to social work as a political profession, for example, being anti-racist;

- ability to navigate interprofessional practice contexts and uphold social work perspectives in the interests of people, their families and communities;
- strengthening professional identity and contributing to the knowledge and practice of social work;
- active involvement in supporting and promoting other social workers' learning;
- use of in-depth understanding of theory, research (including active involvement in) and knowledge from the lived experiences of people in generic and specialist social work practice areas.

These are just some examples of characteristics, and they may not be what you expect to see. You might identify very different aspects of social work practice that you would expect to see or aspire for your career. The SSSC identify Core Learning Elements for all registered social workers, and these will be evidenced in different ways according to the career stage. In effect, wherever you have started from, professional learning seeks to develop your skills and knowledge from that point.

The formal requirements of your CPL

Chapter 1 outlined the current context of social work professional learning noting the history of post-qualifying frameworks and new developments. The evolving context can seem confusing when planning for post-qualifying learning beyond the early career. What remains constant is a drive for acknowledging how social workers deepen and develop their practice through the formal and informal ways that they learn. In 2024, the SSSC revised the CPL requirements for social workers in Scotland with some important changes that remind us that practice is at the core. One of the main changes is that instead of a focus on a number of set hours in a set registration period, the CPL requirements now focus on quality of learning and specific content. An annual declaration is required to confirm that social workers continue to meet their registration requirements and have undertaken CPL in line with core learning elements.

Social workers are also required to ensure that they have undertaken learning about understanding trauma, the wellbeing and protection of children and of adults (SSSC, 2024a). The specific nature of social workers' CPL is argued by the SSSC to be commensurate with their statutory role and protected title. The SSSC highlight that learning can take many forms and they set out a series of principles (SSSC, 2024a) which are centred on peoples' lives. Employer responsibilities for supporting professional learning remain strongly identified in the Codes of Practice (SSSC, 2024b) and the NQSW Supported Year (SSSC, 2024c). As mentioned throughout the book, checking into the SSSC information and resources is recommended to ensure you are clear and aware of current requirements.

The SSSC have developed an interactive CPL website on which you can select the specific kind of information and resources that you need (SSSC, 2024d). This enables you to select, for example, if you are an NQSW or a social worker returning to practice to guide you with the specific expectations of your CPL. The NQSW Supported Year is built on a series of eight Core Learning Elements, and these now also form the basis of CPL beyond that stage. Within the interactive SSSC CPL web pages, you will be able to identify relevant learning activities and resources across these Core Learning Elements.

The Core Learning Elements for Social Workers are:

- ethics, values and rights-based practice;
- communication, engagement and relationship-based professional practice;
- critical thinking, professional judgement and decision-making;
- promoting wellbeing, support and protection;
- working with complexity in unpredictable and ambiguous contexts;
- use of knowledge, research and evidence in practice;
- self-awareness and reflexivity;
- professional leadership.

(SSSC, 2024a)

Specific areas of CPL as your career progresses

If you work in a focused practice field, your CPL is likely to align with this; for example, if working in adoption and fostering services, you might be focused on updating your legal knowledge and innovation in support for children, parents and carers. If you work in substance use, you might be updating or specialising in treatment interventions, new policy and awareness of emerging trends in supply and the effects for those you are working with. The specific partnership context is also something that is important for many social workers' CPL. This chapter provides very brief details of some options with links to where more information can be found. Social workers in your network will inspire you to think about the right options for you. You can also see what some other social workers recommend in the final section of this book.

Specialist training – Mental Health Officer Award

Training as a Mental Health Officer (MHO) is an advanced professional qualification run through universities and partnerships with employers. The trends in numbers of MHOs across Scotland are reported on each year in the workforce data (SSSC, 2024e). When thinking about CPL, the opportunity to train as an MHO is considered by many social workers in Scotland who have an interest in this area of practice. Section 32(2) of the Mental Health (Care and Treatment) (Scotland) Act 2003 positions local authorities with a statutory duty to appoint and provide training for MHOs to undertake mandatory responsibilities, enshrined in legislation. MHO qualifications fall under the approved specialist training programmes that are regulated by the SSSC, which means that any courses must satisfy the rules and requirements set by the regulator and offer the opportunity for learners enrolled to meet the standards and practice competences to achieve the Mental Health Officer Award (MHOA) (SSSC, 2007) which is at Scottish Credit and Qualifications Framework (SCQF) Level 11. Training opportunities are only available to qualified social workers currently employed by local authorities, and it is important to find your local contacts to explore how things are supported in your area.

There are several ways that MHOs continue their professional learning, some of which is, of course, through their practice and with their peers. There are also excellent resources developed by the Mental Welfare Commission, an annual conference specific to MHOs run by the Scottish Association of Social Workers and practitioner forums in many part-nership areas. There is a strong community of practice across MHOs, and the SSSC also highlights some of the ongoing learning opportunities (SSSC, 2007).

Specialist training – child protection

Social workers in children and families settings work across a broad range, and there are often specific pathways for learning around legislative processes and child protection tasks. There is a National Framework for Child Protection Learning and Development in Scotland which identifies the knowledge and skills for all workforce groups (Scottish Government, 2024). A new model of National Joint Investigative Interviewing (Scottish Child Interviewing Model (SCIM)) has also been introduced in Scotland (COSLA, 2024), which has been credit rated by the Scottish Police College at SCQF 9, equivalent to a graduate diploma or Professional Development Award. This is aligned with the Vulnerable Witnesses (Criminal Evidence) (Scotland) Act 2019, which created a new rule for child witnesses under 18 and how they provide evidence in court. This is usually a priority CPL area for statutory services in which they will have a plan and route for eligible staff to train.

Specialist training – becoming a practice educator

Becoming a practice educator is an aspiration for many social workers that stems from their own experiences of being supported as a student. For others, this is part of CPL that emerges over time. Often social workers feel apprehensive and excited at the same time in considering this role. At the time of writing, the available courses in Scotland are mostly run by Higher Education Institutions (HEIs) at SCQF Level 10 and SCQF 11 although there are still some Scottish Qualifications Authority (SQA) Centre-approved programmes. Organisations will have different arrangements for how they recruit and support social workers to become practice educators. If you are reading this book, you are probably interested in learning which makes the practice educator option an ideal choice! As part of the programme, practice educators on all qualifying routes need to support learners and assess them against the Standards in Social Work Education.

Most practice educators begin their pathway taking the role of link worker for social work students where they are directly involved in planning and supporting learning, work-ing with practice educators to provide evidence that informs the assessment decision. Local organisations have different arrangements for training and supporting link workers, but you are in high demand if you are interested. We are likely to see the demand for link workers and practice educators continue in Scotland, and therefore, it is hoped that sup-port for their training and development is built into sector plans. This is most certainly at the fore of issues raised within the sector about social work education, the development, availability of high-quality practice learning for students and strengthening the profession. There is always someone to ask about courses, so please follow up with the providers or your colleagues who will know the local arrangements for recruitment and support for social workers entering these programmes.

Specialist training – supervision, mentoring, coaching and leadership development

Given the importance of leadership in social work and supporting the workforce, leadership and other approaches to supporting social workers remain a popular priority for continuing learning. Learning about taking a professional supervision role is also a popular and necessary area of CPL. There are different opportunities for learning across these areas depending on your employing organisation, however there are many open-access resources available as detailed in Chapter 3 as well as accredited programmes, often part of postgraduate-level qualification pathways. The dedicated NQSW website also has a whole suite of supervision materials created specifically for the role of supervising social workers.

Practitioner research

Being research-minded is a core aspect of social work practice, embedded in the standards at qualifying and NQSW stages, and therefore, CPL will often focus on exploring evidence but also actively undertaking research (e.g., British Association of Social Work, BASW). This can span project-based exploration in services to in-depth studies. There is also an exceptionally vibrant community of social work professionals who are engaged in research studies at a doctorate level including on traditional PhD and diverse Professional Doctorate programmes. It is beyond the scope of this book to delve further into the range and alignment of research methodologies relevant to social work practice, but this does not mean it is not an important CPL option. Knowledge generated across this research spectrum contributes to and increases the professional evidence base for social work.

Supporting social workers' learning in the workplace

Learning to be a social worker and continuing to develop is a personal journey that can be enjoyable but also intense. If you are responsible for planning and supporting social workers' professional development in an organisation. Earlier chapters explored the role of human resources practitioners and learning/development leads in the role of supporting social work. CPL is driven by multiple economic and policy aims across professions including social work (Daley and Cervero, 2016). Social workers continually need to 'construct and reconstruct knowledge [and] skills' (Lester and Costley, 2010, p19). This means that the demands of CPL can be complex in a climate of significantly reduced human and financial resources.

Organisational planning for social work professional learning

Given the budget and other restraints on public services, it is a real challenge for organisations to plan for CPL across the diverse workforces that they are responsible for. The context of leadership, learning and workforce development is considered in other chapters of the book, including that understanding the professional needs of social workers is fundamental to legal and ethical requirements for their CPL. Table 7.1 outlines a way to help plan for social workers CPL in the organisational context.

Table 7.1 Strategic planning for social work professional learning in organisations

Priority level	Considerations
1 What learning/training is essential, mandatory or part of regulatory requirements? *This might include SSSC registration, CPL, health and safety-related learning and other essential compliance requirements such as General Data Protection Regulations and their application to practice.*	How many social workers do you have and what do they need to do? Are there any social work-specific requirements that are different to other workforce groups? What are the ways that the learning or training requirements can be delivered most effectively and efficiently? Are there creative, practice-based or holistic ways to do this in services or in the local partnership contexts? What are the total costs for the organisation of the different CPL requirements? Are there clear projections for the future in place?
2 What priority practice-related learning/training is needed in the organisation, for specific teams and for individual social workers? *These might include specialist practice-related knowledge or skills development in line with policy and legislation etc.*	What other organisational or external resources are needed to support the processes? What are the timescales for completion and the processes for how can this be scheduled, supported and monitored? How is information from individual teams and social workers decided and fed into the organisational planning?
3 What are the aspirational learning requirements that are identified by teams or individuals? *These may not be essential but are important to individuals, teams or services.*	Is everyone clear on their responsibilities for the learning, for example, managers, supervisors and social workers? Are the opportunities for any optional CPL and processes for any funding or otherwise clear to social workers? How are planning and resource decisions made that support the whole of the existing and future workforce needs?

A note on frameworks for learning and development

Learning and development frameworks for specific topics continue to be released in the health and social care sector; these span diverse topics and include Child Protection (Scottish Government, 2024), Dementia (Scottish Government, 2021) and Trauma-Informed Practice (Scottish Government *et al.*, 2023), just a few examples. Every framework is important, but they pose a challenge to the holistic enhancement of skills and knowledge for advancing practice, risking fragmentation as noted by Rory in Chapter 3.

Planning your individual CPL

There is usually a natural alignment with registration requirements which focus on safe, effective practice and the professional development of social workers. Meeting professional regulatory requirements can seem daunting, however you are likely to be learning something every day that contributes to your development and you can focus on what is meaningful for you. There are some helpful prompts to support you to plan for your CPL in the reflective questions below.

Reflective questions

What do you need/want to learn

- Which priority areas of learning do you want to focus on in the next 6–12 months?
- Are there any mandatory requirements that need to be met for your registration or employer?
- What are your longer-term aspirations for learning and development?

Who will help you learn?

- Who are the people who can help you learn?
- How can you maximise the opportunities to learn and reflect on learning from lived experiences?
- Where are other social workers in your organisation or network?
- What is important to learn with other professionals?

How will you develop your learning?

- How can you develop generic and specialist skills and knowledge for your practice area?
- What are the challenges regarding resources to support your identified learning goals? How might these be overcome?
- What are the opportunities for you to support other social workers to learn?

The world of CPL is open to you although there are increasing budget restrictions and different arrangements for supporting social workers. In summary, CPL is important for all social workers and an integrated aspect of social work. There are multiple ways that social workers learn to do their extraordinary work including learning in direct practice. Planning for CPL can help social workers focus on their personal priorities, regulatory and organisational requirements. Social workers are highly influential in one another's learning as part of a cohesive learning culture in the profession.

Learning in practice

I don't think you ever stop learning to be a social worker. I think I probably didn't 'learn' to be a social worker until I was in the job in terms of the social worker that I view myself to be I didn't learn to be that until I started work. Learning to be a social worker …it becomes an integrated part of your identity… I think I did a huge amount of learning as a newly qualified worker within an intake statutory setting and for me being very young at the time that probably took away a lot of the normal experiences I would have as a twenty-something.

I've learnt so much and I've developed my craft so well… I don't think there's a single day goes by without learning.

(Danny in Ferguson, 2021, p140)

Summary points

- Professional learning is part of social work for the whole of the career.
- There is guidance on the regulatory requirements for CPL from the SSSC.
- Generic as well as specialist practice is the focus for social workers' CPL.
- Social workers are engaged in diverse learning opportunities to support their practice.

Further reading

A quick view

A short video launched on Social Work Week 2025, on the CPL requirements from the SSSC, will tune you into the requirements for social workers (https://news.sssc.uk.com/news/social-work-week-2025-supporting-your-cpl-journey).

A suite of helpful resources

The dedicated SSSC CPL website and associated pathways tool is the place to go to explore your learning journey (https://learn.sssc.uk.com/cpl/).

A deeper dive

If you are interested in the concepts of lifelong and lifewide learning, then there is a whole suite of material available on https://www.lifewideeducation.uk/ including full texts and visual resources by Norman Jackson.

Please also see the resources section at the end of this book.

References

Barnett, R (2011) 'Lifewide education: A new and transformative concept for higher education', in Jackson, NJ (ed) *Learning for a complex world: A lifewide concept of learning, education and personal development*, Authorhouse, Bloomington, pp. 22–38.

BASW, *Research and knowledge* [online] https://basw.co.uk/policy-practice/research-and-knowledge.

COSLA (2024) *Joint investigative interviews of child victims and witnesses* [online] https://www.cosla.gov.uk/about-cosla/our-teams/children-and-young-people/joint-investigative-interviews-of-child-victims-and-witnesses.

Daley, BJ and Cervero, RM (2016) 'Learning as the basis for continuing professional education', *New Directions for Adult and Continuing Education*, (151): 19–29, https://doi.org/10.1002/ace.20192.

Ferguson, G (2021) '"When David Bowie created Ziggy Stardust" The lived experiences of social workers learning through work', Doctor of Education (EdD) Thesis, The Open University.

Fisher, J (2012) *Process of personal transition* [online] www.businessballs.com/personalchangeprocess.html.

Grant, S, McCulloch, T, Daly, M and Kettle, M (2022) *Newly qualified social workers in Scotland: A five-year longitudinal study final report* [online] https://www.sssc.uk.com/publications/downloads/2025/04/Newly-qualified-social-workers-in-Scotland-a-five-year-longitudinal-study.pdf.

Lester, S and Costley, C (2010) 'Work-based learning at higher education level: Value, practice and critique', *Studies in Higher Education*, 35(5): 561–575, https://doi.org/10.1080/03075070903216635.

McCulloch, T and Taylor, S (2018) 'Becoming a social worker: Realising a shared approach to professional learning?', *British Journal of Social Work*, 48(8): 2272–2290, https://doi.org/10.1093/bjsw/bcx157.

Moriarty, J, Baginsky, M and Manthorpe, J (2015) *Literature review of roles and issues within the social work profession in England* [online] https://www.professionalstandards.org.uk/docs/default-source/publications/research-paper/literature-review-roles-and-issues-within-the-social-work-profession-in-england-2015.pdf.

Scottish Government (2021) *Promoting* excellence [online] https://www.gov.scot/publications/promoting-excellence-2021-framework-health-social-services-staff-working-people-dementia-families-carers/.

Scottish Government (2024) *Child protection learning and development 2024: National framework* [online] https://www.gov.scot/publications/national-framework-child-protection-learning-development-scotland-2024/.

Scottish Government, NHS Education for Scotland, COSLA, Resilience Learning Partnership and Improvement Service (2023) *A roadmap for creating trauma-informed and responsive change: Guidance for organisations, systems and workforces in Scotland* [online] https://www.traumatransformation.scot/implementation/.

SSSC (2007) *Introduction to the standards and practice competences to achieve Mental Health Officer Award* [online] https://www.sssc.uk.com/about-us/publications/standard-for-mental-health-officer-award/.

SSSC (2024a) *Continuous professional learning* [online] https://www.sssc.uk.com/supporting-the-workforce/continuous-professional-learning/.

SSSC (2024b) *The SSSC codes of practice* [online] https://www.sssc.uk.com/the-scottish-social-services-council/sssc-codes-of-practice/.

SSSC (2024c) *NQSW supported year overview and guidance 2024* [online] https://www.nqsw.sssc.uk.com/resource/nqsw-supported-year-overview-and-guidance/.

SSSC (2024d) *Continuous professional learning for registrants* [online] https://learn.sssc.uk.com/cpl/.

SSSC (2024e) *Mental Health Officers (Scotland) Report 2023 Scottish Social Services Workforce Data* [online] https://data.sssc.uk.com/data-publications/23-mental-health-officers-reports/357-mental-health-officers-scotland-report-2023.

Part Three

Learning together for effective social work practice

Chapter 8

Cultivating learning environments in social work practice settings

Introduction

The learning environment can include almost everything around a person. Social workers' experiences and theories about learning organisations, cultures and environments can help us understand what matters in these. This chapter explores key issues and ideas for developing, supporting and evaluating practice learning opportunities in social services, with the learning environment as a central factor. The theory and practice of creating inclusive, effective environments for learning is a core taught element of practice educator training but extends to all professionals. Drawing from theoretical principles applied to social work settings, the role of practice educators and other colleagues is explored. This chapter explores effective learning environments at the individual, team and organisational level linked with conceptions of leadership for learning (see Chapter 3). The discussion also considers the diversity of settings for practice learning in integrated, partnership contexts.

Chapter aims

By the end of the chapter, you will be able to:

- describe the essential elements of an effective, inclusive learning environment;
- identify the opportunities and barriers to learning in organisations you know;
- plan and evaluate ethical learning environments for social work.

What is a learning environment?

The learning environment is often thought about as the direct space or place that a learner occupies, their desk, their equipment or the team area that they are sitting in within a workplace. When teams and practice educators are preparing for a student to come, they will think about this physical environment and include details on agency profiles and learning agreements. The learning environment is much broader than this immediate physical space and can be thought of as more of a landscape (Wenger-Trayner and Wenger-Traynor, 2015) in which certain elements will either foster learning or inhibit it. The quality of the learning environment is fundamental to whether social workers will learn, particularly when they are being assessed in their practice

DOI: 10.4324/9781041057598-12

(Wareing and Ferguson, 2024). It is also important not only to think about social work students in terms of learning cultures and the opportunities therein. The overall learning culture within social work teams and organisations and across partnerships is essential for learning at all career stages. To think about social workers' learning, it is essential to think of the specific nature of the landscape of social work services and how this can promote learning.

Supporting learning in a social services context

The curriculum of practice learning qualifications in Scotland highlights the specific nature of supporting learning in a social services context and creating environments for learning. Wareing and Ferguson (2024) depict the learning environment of health and social care in a visual mind map, which shows that learning in this context is very different to other work settings. People who use social work services are at the heart of the learning environment, and practitioners are positioned centrally with a reminder that we all have diverse tasks, roles, motivation and personal and professional backgrounds (Wareing and Ferguson, 2024). The landscape of practice is characterised by physical and non-physical elements. For example, legislation or policy that influences our lives, which services are funded, their priorities and any associated regulations, frameworks, practice guidance and procedures are part of the learning context. Policy also directly influences the resources that are available for resourcing of learning and development. Service demands and constraints are a challenge for organisations and learners within them in relation to trying to balance delivery of services while managing staff shortages, funding cuts and increasing demands.

Reflective questions

- What do you think are the most important elements of a learning environment?
- To what extent does organisational culture influence learning in settings that you are familiar with?
- How can individual learning be supported in social work environments?

Social work expertise, practice wisdom, frameworks, guidance and procedures all influence the learning environment and focus of learning. Relationships that promote and support learning, including interprofessional relationships, are also central to the social work learning environment and discussed fully in Chapter 9. Learning to work within integrated settings, multi-agency partnerships, navigating communication-sharing dilemmas, referral arrangements and working in constrained services are just some of the expectations of practice. Compassionate, inclusive and anti-oppressive learning cultures mirror the skills, values and ethics of care services. These include safe, reflective learning spaces, values and ethics and promote social justice in their inclusive design.

We have explored some initial ideas about learning in workplace settings and specific issues influencing health and social care contexts, but it is important to now turn to focus on who creates the learning environment. People at the individual, team, organisational and strategic sector leaders all have a role in promoting, creating and sustaining learning environments.

Organisational cultures that promote and support social workers' learning

A profession which at its heart is concerned with understanding the individual within the context of their experiences and which aims to challenge inequality, social work organisations have readily embraced the theories of learning organisations and cultures. Yorke and Knight (2004) suggest that there is a distinctive set of educational practices for a subject like social work, such as experiential and problem-based approaches. Social work has been rooted in these types of approaches to learning, recognising that there is no simplistic transfer of knowledge from education that can equip practitioners for the role. Moon (2000) is clear that an egalitarian environment is a prerequisite for critical reflection, a further essential ingredient of social work professional development. While the rhetoric is strong in social work, the reality of social workers' experience of learning organisations is not always so (Beddoe, 2009; Grant et al., 2022; McCulloch et al., 2024).

Theories about learning cultures

Organisational psychology, theories and practices related to learning cultures, and how learning is embedded in what an organisation does, continue to be a focus of work in the Human Resource (HR) professional domain (CIPD, 2020). Often linked with business models and organisations, guidance from the Chartered Institute of Personnel and Development (CIPD) is a rich source of reference and resource for public services too. Barends and Rousseau (2022) suggest that a definition of organisational culture is elusive but includes shared underlying norms, assumptions and collectively held history of an organisation. Culture can also be referred to as the way things are done, often visible to newcomers but not always in the consciousness of those who have been immersed. Barends and Rousseau remind us that organisational climate is also conceptualised as how people experience and perceive practices and procedures. Edgar Schein's work is also commonly cited in identifying three aspects of organisational culture: 'underlying assumptions and beliefs, that may be conscious or unconscious; norms and values about appropriate attitudes and behaviours, that may be espoused or real; and artefacts that may reflect these, for example, symbols and language' (Schein in Barends and Rousseau, 2022, p6).

Learning organisations

Conceptions of learning organisations stemming from the work of Peter Senge have also been widely used in social work and broader social service development. These were integrated into and a key component of the vision of the suite of Scottish practice learning qualifications introduced in the 2000s. Senge defines a learning organisation as

> a place where people continually expand their capacity to create the results they truly desire, where new and expansive patterns of thinking are nurtured, where collective aspiration is set free, and where people are continually learning to see the whole (reality) together.
>
> (Senge, 2006, p3)

Within a learning organisation, the principles, practices and essences are part of a system that enables learning.

Senge identifies five disciplines of a learning organisation:

- systems thinking;
- personal mastery;
- mental models;
- building shared vision;
- team learning.

Senge is interested in practices (what we do), principles (guiding ideas) and essences (the personal disciplines that influence the system). Closely aligned with leadership approaches, authentic vision is deeply linked with an ethical purpose. Reflective practices at individual and organisational level or feedback loops (Argyris and Schön, 1978) are fundamental to learning in the system. It is beyond the scope of this chapter to fully explore Senge's ideas, and the ideas can be oversimplified or misunderstood. Theory of the learning organisation, human nature and learning systems are closely aligned with the ideas discussed in Chapter 3 and the work of Otto Scharmer. Indeed, Senge and Scharmer are two of the authors of the text *Presence: An Exploration of Profound Change in People, Organizations, and Society.*

Learning in practice

In the practice environment social workers were having less opportunity to be with other social workers. Some local authorities and partnerships also don't have anybody in a specific social work learning or development role anymore. Often strategically people are reliant on traditional models of when these were vibrant posts across the whole network in Scotland. Research showed that lots of significant learning was down to chance which is just should not be. There is a window of time now, in relation to seeing the system and aligning the planets, but this will go by and we can miss the opportunity.

(Mark, Learning and Development Workforce lead)

Creating learning environments

Social workers and educators will often think about steps to creating a learning organisation. Learning environments are dynamic, and the title of the chapter uses the term 'cultivate' to indicate possibilities of growth, nurture and development. Chapter 3 explored the concept of learning ecosystems or ecologies, suggesting that these are complex adaptive systems in which different elements influence one another positively or negatively.

Human learning systems (Lowe, 2020) is an approach to development which embraces the complexity of public services, key organisational change and systems thinking theories. Within this approach, ideas of system stewardship and systems convenors are central to pushing across traditional silos to harness the potential learning capabilities within the landscape (Wenger-Traynor and Wenger-Traynor, 2021). A social work professional learning ecosystem needs people who understand and see the complexity of the landscape for learning and agitate for change in the places where they have power to do so. Scotland also has an evolving drive to support system and service development using design principles (Scottish Government, 2019) which have people who use services at the centre. Design thinking is woven into service improvement expectations and the self-evaluation approaches embedded in the Care Inspectorate scrutiny. Approaches to taking an eco-system approach to thinking about professional learning for social work can therefore be supported by the ideology and tools which are widely available.

Exploring and reviewing learning opportunities, cultures and organisations

Some great resources were developed as part of the former Scottish Practice Learning Project, in the Scottish Organisation of Practice Teachers (ScOPT) and within different organisations to explore and audit quality practice learning. The Social Care Institute for Excellence (SCIE) also produced a fantastic resource pack on developing learning organisations which was widely used in the former Tayforth Practice Learning programme. It can be helpful to think about the system in which different types of opportunity are delivered to be able to review how the organisational culture influences social workers' learning.

Table 8.1 Learning organisations and cultures audit tool

Key characteristics of a learning organisation	Focused questions to support development
Organisational structure Participation and feedback are actively sought, valued and used to influence and inform practice, including from people using the services. Learning from and using the expertise of teams and individuals is integral. Learning across the organisation and wider partnerships is collaborative.	Which systems are in place that gather, analyse and act on feedback? What is the level of understanding, commitment and resourcing of co-production and learning with service users and carers? How do social workers share practice issues and learning together? What does the organisation do to understand or use the range of skills, knowledge and expertise across teams and the wider organisation/partnerships?
Organisational culture There are shared beliefs, values and goals in line with the fundamental aims of social work. Creativity and innovation are encouraged; learning from mistakes and testing new ways of working are embedded. Use of evidence and research are critically evaluated and used to inform practice.	How accessible and meaningful are the organisation's policies, values and approaches? What ways does everyone contribute to shaping the beliefs and values? Does the rhetoric of any written statements match the reality for people? What are the barriers to new ideas being considered? How are changes planned, managed and reviewed? Is effective practice celebrated and shared throughout the organisation? What is the attitude to risk-taking and learning from things that have not gone well? How is research and other evidence generated, used and shared in the organisation, including how this underpins policy/guidance? Is there a culture of practitioner research?

(Continued)

Table 8.1 (Continued)

Key characteristics of a learning organisation	Focused questions to support development
Information systems Communication and information systems are effective within and across the organisation and to the external environment. Policies and procedures are understood by everyone and are based on human rights and social justice.	How is information communicated well or otherwise in teams and the wider organisation, both formally and informally? Are information and communication channels with partner organisations effective? Are the policies and guidance rooted in human rights and social justice?
HR practices Continuing professional learning is embedded in practices and incorporates the needs of professional social workers. Professional supervision is integrated in a cohesive system that supports learning and development.	How is professional supervision embedded in the policies and practices in all teams? Is continuing professional learning an embedded and encouraged aspect of organisational practices? If so how? What is done to ensure continuing professional learning opportunities are equitable, accessible and inclusive to all social workers' learning needs and styles? How does the organisation support the regulatory requirements of social workers' continuing professional learning?
Leadership There is capacity for the organisation to reflect, change and improve. Leadership at all levels is encouraged.	How is leadership for social work distributed across all levels of the organisation? What are the informal and formal leadership development opportunities for social workers? Who contributes to an effective learning culture in the organisation?

Source: Adapted from SCIE (2004).

Evaluating learning environments

Crucial to the success of any learning environment is the review and evaluation cycle which uses feedback to inform improvement. Kirkpatrick and Kirkpatrick (2006) remind us that in designing a learning opportunity, we should focus on the overall desired result of that initiative and then plan how this can be achieved. To measure any desired changes, increased skills or knowledge, it is necessary to understand the baseline of an individual, service or team. This includes specifically considering what learners need to learn to achieve those ultimate learning outcomes. The Kirkpatrick model has four interconnected levels, all of which are important:

Reactions

This is a common focus of evaluation, the focus on how a learner has directly experienced a learning event or programme. Typically, this provides great feedback on how valuable the learning event has seemed in terms of relevance and enjoyment, however it is unclear from this how the learning will influence direct practice or outcomes for people in social work services.

Learning

Identifying specific learning that is a result of an event or initiative might involve checking what specific knowledge or skills have been developed through this stage of evaluation. In some cases, people will measure reactions and learning by seeking feedback through questionnaires, comments or follow-up discussion. Having a well-designed learning opportunity will have anticipated outcomes that are clearly identified, and it is these that will be evaluated.

Behaviours

How learning develops social work practice skills is harder to measure as part of a comprehensive evaluation strategy. What is changing about the confidence of social workers and their ability to use learning in their practice is the focus of this level. Most often this is reviewed through follow-up questionnaires but can be integrated effectively in supervision discussion in a well-designed programme or learning organisation.

Results

How practice is enhanced and the outcomes of that for social work is traditionally much harder to measure than results and perceptions of learning. If learning goals are clearly identified and indicators of change are considered in the learning design, then evidence might helpfully be drawn from social workers, managers, service users and partner organisations. While this is a complex aspect of evaluation, the results of learning are increasingly important to target resources that will enhance priority areas of practice.

Reflective questions

- What would be included in a creative evaluation strategy for social workers' learning?
- Where would there be evidence of effective learning?
- Who would provide important evidence to support the evaluation cycle?

Too often the idea of evaluation is an afterthought in relation to learning, and building a clear evaluation strategy into programmes is essential. Beyond the simplistic overview of different levels, it is also important that the right people are involved in planning and evaluation throughout the process for learning to be effective. The Kirkpatrick model of learning evaluation has been integrated into teaching in Scottish practice education qualifications for many years. The model is also included in the National Framework for Child Protection Learning and Development in Scotland (Scottish Government, 2024) along with a concise summary in the appendices. The Kirkpatrick model is rare in its focus specifically on evaluating learning as opposed to service outcomes, albeit these have started to have a much stronger connection in organisational review. Incredibly creative approaches to evaluating outcomes in complex public service systems are at the fore of Morton and Cook (2022) who embrace the social, political and partnership influences on making a difference to people in caring systems. Within the context of complex systems, individual and wider sector learning is essential to growth.

A learning environment is 'expansive or restrictive' in the opportunities that it affords or enables within it (Engeström, 2001). Chapter 6 outlined some of the places and spaces in which social work learning happens including the physical, psychological and cultural elements. Specific aspects of the Scottish geographic landscape were also acknowledged. All these aspects of the learning environment can lead to inequalities opportunities available to social workers. Mapping learning opportunities across the landscape can help develop more of a cohesive approach professional learning in Scotland.

Learning in practice

There's a big relationship between the learning opportunity and the therapeutic support that comes with it. It almost as if they feed each other and feed the relationships across the system. If we acknowledge that's the way we're doing it, it naturally encourages conversation around that, which is learning for everyone in that sense. When I thought about the web diagram about social workers' learning I thought 'Aha!' because it explained what was always in my head, all the components of the web, I understood all the bits and where they sit in terms of wellbeing and looking after workers but also understood some of that links to how we can professionally develop workers in the right way. The supervision, social workers themselves, the feedback loops, connections across managers and partnerships all feed the learning system.

(Alan, Learning and Development Workforce lead)

Reflective questions

- How would you define a learning organisation?
- What are the opportunities for strengthening the learning environment for social workers in Scotland?
- What opportunities do you have to help strengthen cultures for learning?

Summary of key points

- Understanding learning environments is essential for professional learning.
- Learning cultures are underpinned by core social work values and skills.
- Leadership for learning is at the heart of strengthening learning environments.
- Strengthening the professional learning system in Scotland is essential for sustaining social work.

Further reading

A quick read

For a quick summary of Peter Senge's ideas (and many other theories!), I'd recommend going to *infed.org* the Encyclopaedia of Pedagogy and Informal Education which is curated by the informal education and community action leading authority Mark K. Smith.

A creative guide

You can find an easy to read summary and creative tools related to Kirkpatrick's evaluation framework on the internet site www.*businessballs.com* along with some other great material from Leslie Rae on evaluating learning.

A deeper dive

I would really highlight Wenger-Traynor and colleagues (book *Learning in Landscapes of Practice* for anyone who wants to think more about this. Also if anyone is interested in all things learning communities and systems, Beverley and Etienne Wenger-Traynor's international resources are here: https://www.wenger-trayner.com/.

Please also see the resources section in the Appendix.

References

Argyris, C and Schön, D (1978) *Organizational learning: A theory of action perspective*, Addison Wesley, Massachusetts.

Barends, E and Rousseau, D (2022) *Organisational culture and performance: An evidence review, scientific summary*, Chartered Institute of Personnel and Development, London.

Beddoe, L (2009) 'Creating continuous conversation: Social workers and learning organizations', *Social Work Education*, 28(7): 722–736, https://doi.org/10.1080/02615470802570828.

CIPD (2020) *Creating learning cultures: Assessing the evidence*, Chartered Institute of Personnel and Development, London.

Engeström, Y (2001) 'Expansive learning at work: Toward an activity theoretical reconceptualization', *Journal of Education and Work*, 14(1): 133–156, https://doi.org/10.1080/13639080020028747.

Grant, S, McCulloch, T, Daly, M and Kettle, M (2022) *Newly qualified social workers in Scotland: A five-year longitudinal study final report* [online] https://www.sssc.uk.com/publications/downloads/2025/04/Newly-qualified-social-workers-in-Scotland-a-five-year-longitudinal-study.pdf.

Kirkpatrick, D and Kirkpatrick, J (2006) *Evaluating training programs: The four levels*, Berrett-Koehler, San Francisco.

Lowe, T (2020) *A human, learning, systems approach* [online] https://www.humanlearning.systems/theory/.

McCulloch, T, Grant, S, Daly, M, Sen, R and Ferguson, G (2024) 'Embedding learning as a practice of value: Learning from the experiences of early career social workers in Scotland', *The British Journal of Social Work*, 54 (7): 2977–2995, https://doi.org/10.1093/bjsw/bcae072.

Moon, J (2000) *Reflection in learning & professional development: Theory & practice*, Routledge, London.

Morton, S and Cool, A (2022) *How do you know if you are making a difference? A practical handbook for public service organisations*, Policy Press, Bristol.

SCIE (2004) *Learning organisations: a self assessment resource pack*, Social Care Institute for Excellence, Egham.

Scottish Government (2019) *The Scottish approach to service design* [online] https://www.gov.scot/publications/the-scottish-approach-to-service-design/.

Scottish Government (2024) *Child protection learning and development 2024: National framework* [online] https://www.gov.scot/publications/national-framework-child-protection-learning-development-scotland-2024/.

Senge, PM (2006) *The fifth discipline: The art and practice of the learning organization*, Random House, London.

Wareing, M and Ferguson, G (2024) 'Learning environments', in Wareing, M (ed) *Practice supervision and assessment in nursing, health and social care*, Routledge, Abingdon, pp. 27–39.

Wenger-Trayner, E and Wenger-Traynor, B (2015) 'Learning in a landscape of practice: A framework', in Wenger-Traynor, E, Fenton-O'Creevy, M, Hutchinson, S, Kubiak, C and Wenger-Trayner, B (eds) *Learning in landscapes of practice: Boundaries, identity, and knowledgeability in practice-based learning*, Routledge, London, pp. 2–15.

Wenger-Traynor, E, and Wenger-Traynor, B (2021) *Systems convening, a crucial form of leadership for the 21st century* [online] https://www.wenger-trayner.com/wp-content/uploads/2021/09/Systems-Convening.pdf.

Yorke, M and Knight, P (2004) 'Self-theories: Some implications for teaching and learning in higher education', *Studies in Higher Education*, 29(1): 25–37, https://doi.org/10.1080/1234567032000164859.

Chapter 9

Effective relationships for social work practice learning

Introduction

This chapter explores why relationships matter for social workers' learning. Learning with other people is central to social work professional development at all career stages. This chapter centralises the importance of learning from the lived experience of people who use social work services. Involving people with lived experience in social workers' professional learning, including the learning and assessment of social work students, is essential.

Developing effective relationships to supervise, facilitate and assess the learning of individual students is discussed drawing on examples and expertise from the practice learning community in Scotland. This chapter also considers the wider relationships across teams, organisations and partnerships which influence learning.

Chapter aims

By the end of the chapter, you will be able to:

- describe the range of relationships that support social workers' learning;
- understand how people who use services inform learning and assessment;
- identify opportunities for strengthening relationships for learning.

What relationships matter for professional learning?

Human relationships are well known to be at the heart of effective social work practice and the basis for any intervention (Ruch et al., 2018). Ingram and Smith (2018) provide an excellent summary, linked to Scottish context, of the philosophical, policy and practice rationale for why relationships are fundamental for social work. A revival of therapeutic practice continues to emerge in the Scottish context. Establishing effective learning relationships is a core requisite of the social work practice educator curriculum and an essential feature of learning environments and learning ecologies. Part One of this book highlighted that everyone is a learner, an educator and a leader in social work within a professional learning ecosystem. Relationships at individual, team, organisational and wider partnership levels influence learning in many ways. Bringing an awareness to relationships that matter for learning can help us focus on strengthening these. Relationships as part of a healthy learning environment provide a supportive net for safe, reflective spaces with learners and educators having a key role contributing to how this is created.

DOI: 10.4324/9781041057598-13

Relationships between people are the most important aspect of an expansive learning environment (Wareing and Ferguson, 2024).

The importance of relationships in the Scottish context

Relationships are front and centre for learning in the Scottish social work standards (SSSC, 2019), implicit throughout and explicit in key parts, for example:

- Develop relationships with people who show respect for diversity, equality, dignity, confidentiality and privacy (SiSWE 2.3).
- Work collaboratively with people to identify, explore and evaluate support networks that can be accessed and developed (SiSWE 2.5).
- Develop effective helping relationships and partnerships with key people that strengthen communities, to bring about change and achieve planned outcomes (SiSWE 2.5).
- I will form open, positive relationships and maintain professional boundaries with individuals, colleagues or carers who respect their dignity, wellbeing and safety (Codes of Practice 2.8).
- I will not form unprofessional or harmful relationships with individuals or carers (Codes of Practice 6.3).
- Work effectively with others to demonstrate the contribution of social work in delivering integrated and multidisciplinary services (SiSWE 5.6).
- Complex tensions in intra-personal and inter-personal relationships and processes (SiSWE 5.6).
- Act in a professional manner, with appropriate use of self, in management of relationships (SiSWE 5.6).

Relationships are not static but a powerful, dynamic force shaped by the people therein. Communication, engagement and relationship-based professional practice is Core Learning Element 2 in the Newly Qualified Social Worker (NQSW) Core Learning Elements (SSSC, 2024a). There are expectations of developing and deepening relationships in practice, acknowledging professional authority. Inclusion, respect and ethical practice are enacted through the social work relationship, developing 'skills to manage professional relationships, boundaries and endings with integrity, care, compassion and respect' (SSSC, 2024a, p8). The NQSW guidance also details many aspects of how social workers' learning is fundamentally related to self and relationships-based practice in 'highly charged and complex situations' (SSSC, 2024a, p7). Although these are just some examples of how relationships are woven into the fabric of social work practice, the details are carefully considered and informed by the experience of the Scottish sector which remains strongly rooted in rights-based, trauma-informed approaches. It is striking that this aspect of practice continues to strengthen in the formal requirements for professional practice in Scotland. For social workers' professional learning, relationships are also at the heart.

Learning from lived experiences and relationships with people

In Navigating Evidence (Vallely, 2020), lived experiences are positioned as a key source for evidence informed practice. Learning from lived experiences has been at the fore of social work education for decades, another key area of enquiry in the review of the Standards in Social Work Education (SiSWE), but this does not mean that it has become fully embedded. Challenges remain in recognition of the fundamental need to involve people in social workers' professional learning and resourcing of this critical component (Duffy and Beresford, 2020). Work in some Scottish universities has nonetheless been inspirational to name two of many examples: co-production of skills development in the University of Stirling Unity group (Bell *et al.*, 2020) and the caring experience in Dundee University where students spend 24 hours with an individual or family (Gee *et al.*, 2009). In the Open University, and across other Higher Education Institutions (HEIs), people who have lived experiences of social work services are involved in the design and review of module content, a core contributor to the interview and recruitment process alongside being involved in research and development initiatives. Arrangements for how this work is resourced and individuals are remunerated remains a hot topic of debate and concern with no clear and consistent pattern. Evidence continues to generate that inspiring conversations are fundamental to social work education, and that user involvement is both meaningful and demonstrates learning outcomes for practice (Cabiati and Levy, 2021; Levy *et al.*, 2021).

Reflective questions

- What value is placed in learning from lived experiences in your practice setting or one that you are familiar with?
- How are people using your service involved in the learning and assessment of social work students and qualified social workers?
- Where are the opportunities for people using services to influence social workers' learning and development?

Daniel Piggins has worked with people all his adult life. As a member of the Open University service user and carer group, Daniel has been active in driving a customer-focused approach to involvement in social work education for many years. Working collaboratively with colleagues, Daniel is part of a team who is central to the student journey including recruitment and development of the curriculum. Daniel describes that he lives independently with a severe visual impairment. In conversation with Daniel, he states that the question that is most frequently asked is 'Why is it considered good practice, or indeed best practice to involve people with lived experience in social work education?'. This question is asked by everyone from casually interested bystanders to senior professionals whose job is to manage social work. The answer, Daniel suggests, is refreshingly simple: drawing on a customer service analogy, people are always being asked for feedback in all areas of life. Some people will pay lip service to this, but others really care.

Daniel described the analogy of Irn Bru to elaborate. The people who make Irn Bru, when the sugar tax came in, their product, sales and customer satisfaction were hit when their recipe was changed (Moncur, 2019). The makers of the drink listened to many dissatisfied customers and brought out a new, premium product as an initial limited addition which subsequently became a mainstream offer. Daniel suggests this is an excellent example of an organisation listening to customers. Bringing these ideas back to social work, Daniel suggests that although social work is unlikely to go out of business, it is essential to listen to people who use because the people who use it are the people who will keep it going. Daniel highlights how the costs associated with involving people in social work education and practice are not always recognised in line with their actual value. While the cost may not look good on a balance sheet, it is a crucial component of user satisfaction.

Based on his experiences, Daniel suggests ten essential ingredients for effective relationships with and involvement of people with lived experiences of social work services in social workers' learning.

Daniel's ten essential ingredients for effective involvement

1 If you are going to involve us, then do it properly.
2 If you are considering a career in social work or if you are involved in care work, and you would like to develop, before you jump in with both feet and find yourself out of your depth, talk to your clients; they are at the end of the day your customers.
3 Show your service users, if you involve them, the same respect that you would want for anybody else. We are not a toy that you can just pick up, play with for five minutes and then put down. We are people who know how the system works, we have been in it, have observed it or are likely to use it, and you absolutely must show us the respect for that. Nothing is worse than being paid lip service to.
4 For people who are already in the profession. Do not under any circumstances make your first contact with me, my nearest and dearest, or my friends and family; turn into a preconceived set agenda about how you are going to rush in and solve my problem.
5 Do not just tick the boxes and generate paper as this is not helpful. You will be disadvantaged because you will not have taken the time. If it becomes a box-ticking exercise, it becomes pointless. It is about the involvement and consultation. The client may as well use an artificial intelligence (AI) robot to self-serve.
6 The system currently is sufficiently cumbersome that we need, regardless of whether we want it or not, 'the paper-clip scrutiny committee'; there is a lot of time and money wasted. If you reimagine and really focus on authentic customer engagement, the system becomes less wasteful.
7 Advice to anyone in social work from whatever route that has led them there; be open to anything in terms of learning.
8 You need to always be learning, growing and open to change.
9 There is no manual needed but a set of objectives and how you meet them is helpful. The danger of an AI robot would be that it would follow a rule book and that is the day that social work dies because there can't be a relationship if there is no human. How can I as a service user, or an educator, or a contributor to interviews have a relationship with a book of rules?
10 If you mess up, admit that you messed up; otherwise, the relationship is ruined. This is so important. To me it is more important that you are honest. I can train you to be a good listener, your peers can train you to be a good social worker, but if you mak a munsie o' it* and got it wrong, admit this, and that starts with the client.

Daniel Piggins
* *to mak a munsie o'*, of persons or things: to reduce to a ridiculous or sorry condition, to spoil, make a mess of, botch, bungle (Dictionaries of the Scots Language)

There are many things that can perhaps only be learned from people's experiences (Wareing and Ferguson, 2024), something central to the human library concept which values this expertise (Giesler, 2021). Every person will have their own individual experiences and views on how effective learning relationships can be developed, an important reflective point throughout the career.

Learning through other social workers

Learning with and through other people repeatedly features as one of the most important sources for professional learning (Ferguson, 2021), and this happens in practice settings. Social workers need other social workers as an essential ingredient in their professional learning (Ferguson, 2022), and yet the spaces where social workers can be together have diminished in relation to agile working and changes in the physical location of teams (Grant et al., 2022). Social workers describe learning through the teams that they are in, through challenging discussions and with colleagues as hugely important. Learning about different approaches to practice happens in social workers' relationships. The Scottish Social Services Council (SSSC) resources for the NQSW Supported Year include ideas for structured peer learning (SSSC, 2024b), and the Scottish Association for Social Workers (SASW) delivers many peer-led services. The role of team managers, practice educators and link workers is also recognised in their influence on the learning culture. Motivation of other social workers plays a key part in professional learning.

Social workers' contribution to the learning of others has been established in the SSSC Codes of Practice since their inception and a highly valued component of continuing professional learning (CPL): (I identify opportunities to learn from and share learning with others CPL Principle 3). When there have been difficult practice encounters or outcomes, shared learning is often potent. The issues raised by Daniel in summary of the importance of involving and learning from people's lived experiences are aligned with social workers' perspectives. Specific, nuanced learning outcomes for social workers have arisen from their practice in this respect as shown in Table 9.1.

Table 9.1 Important learning points in social work practice relationships

Learning about the impact of previous decisions about children
Learning about different disabilities and how these impact on daily life
Learning that people should be given more of a chance
Learning about the importance of the relationship and just being there
Learning from watching children experiencing pure joy
Learning about the legacy of trauma, the impact of abuse and neglect
Learning how people can be perceived and demonised
Learning about the importance of listening
Learning about freedom, humanity and challenging discrimination
Learning that children's lives are complex and chaotic, characterised by the past and the present
Learning about powerful non-verbal communication
Learning to be honest and straightforward with people
Learning about the importance of really getting to know people
Learning about the impact of a simple task on a person's whole life
The impact of learning from a simple task for the whole of the career
Learning about the importance of respect
Learning how to respond to people
Learning through the senses

Source: Adapted from Ferguson (2021).

Learning in practice

This was actually real and a real person's life, I think what was a wee bit over-whelming was the ordinariness of the family, it was like going into my mum and dad's house and you suddenly thought, 'oh wait a minute – this is social work' ... every family's got a story, you know the uniqueness of their life, and it's us, you know, we're all a step away from situations, whether it's drugs and alcohol or mental health, you know, it's us.

Kathleen in Ferguson (2021, p110)

Learning with other professionals

Learning with other professionals in different disciplines has been promoted over time, featuring in the review of the SiSWE and subsequent publications (e.g., Bolger, 2019). Given the nature of policy, practice and legislation, such as the Public Bodies (Joint Working) (Scotland) Act (2014) and the Children and Young People (Scotland) Act (2014) taking an explicit focus on partnership and integration, this is no surprise. While there is a huge value in learning together, there are some risks unless there is sufficient safe space for social workers to learn with one another about social work and the specific developmental issues for the role. Accounts from the lived experiences of social workers reveal interesting details about what they have learned in multi-agency learning arenas and what they have learned from other professionals in practice examples. Social workers described their experience of conflict with other professionals with power dynamics shaping relationships and practice outcomes (Simpson *et al.*, 2017; Ferguson, 2021).

Working within a multi-agency context is central to expectations of social workers (Ferguson, 2021). For example, Sophie learned about the importance of partnership approaches but also learned that she felt solely responsible as a social worker for holding risk where children were placed on the Child Protection Register although 'everybody was signed up to want to really support this family' but 'the whole multi-agency approach can be lost in cases where there is crisis work' (Sophie in Ferguson, 2021, p112). Kathleen also reflected on the importance of learning from the different professions, including other social workers in multi-agency teams. Learning with other social workers does not conflict with the importance and intentions of interprofessional learning. In an interprofessional context, it is even more vital that there is opportunity to strengthen learning with different colleagues (Ferguson, 2021).

Reflective questions

- Which assumptions are made about social workers and other professionals? List a few examples.
- What do we bring from our training and practice that will help or hinder our working relationships?
- Why does the context of interprofessional relationships matter for effective learning?

You might have a clear understanding of different professions based on your experience or have reflected on blurred boundaries between roles. Perhaps you have experience of very effective multi-agency working that has helped you learn.

Strengthening relationships for learning

Power and privilege always need to be considered in individual, team, organisation and partnership contexts. As with most privilege, those who hold this can be unaware. Individual and organisational defense mechanisms can also get in the way of productive, open and honest relationships. While working as a learning and development advisor, I undertook an informal audit of final placement practice learning. This led to consider how using explosive metaphors could shine light on the intensity of relationships in practice learning, particularly when things go wrong. One of the most complex issues to manage in practice learning is when a student is not on track for a pass recommendation in an assessed placement. The impact of failing social work placements on all the people involved has been widely acknowledged (Eno and Kerr 2013; Finch, 2017) in terms of the resource, stress and ongoing legacy on people and services. In contrast, Schaub and Dalrymple also provide accounts of the joy and appreciation of student's contributions when things go well. Alongside these polar perspectives, Eno and Kerr (2013) suggest that there can be such a thing as a good fail and opportunity for enhanced learning reliant on how things are managed. Setting a careful foundation for assessing learning is explored more fully in Chapter 10.

Students as educators – developing relationships in a different way

An innovative initiative in the Tayforth Partnership delivery of the Practice Learning Qualification (PLQ) between 2017 and 2019 was the integration of an activity that engaged students as educators. This initiative was developed in partnership with a creative university lecturer, Dr Ann Hodson, and students on their final placement based in a local authority context. The focus of the activity was on understanding and strengthening relationships through collaboration. The aim of the project was to provide students with an opportunity to research existing knowledge on group processes and relationships and apply this to practice learning relationships. The vision was to create new knowledge together within the practice learning community. Students were tasked with researching, designing and delivering a half-day workshop that was part of the teaching input. The task was aligned with the SiSWE so that students could generate and demonstrate evidence for their own assessment in relation to working with groups, exploring research and managing relationships. The design of this initiative was to turn perceived power dynamics around and to learn from those at the receiving end of practice educator support. Within this example, none of the students' own practice educators were present. The sessions were a valuable experience for all with shared learning about experiences of power and the importance of relationships.

Placements are high stakes for students in relation to their aspirations, investment and learning. We are all there for the same reasons in relation to social workers' development, but it does not always feel this way. Practice learning is described as a 'combination of interaction and transaction ... a space of force-relations between agents with different kinds of capital' (Parker, 2008, p995) in which power is negotiated. Eno and Kerr highlight the role of relationships as the vehicle and the arena for brokering this power.

Networks for learning

Multiple relationships can influence the coordination, learning, assessment of practice learning and the longer-term impact and outcomes on all involved. Within any relationship, there are dynamics of passion and power that either enable or are a barrier to learning. When things go wrong in relationships, this involves significant emotional labour, and if unresolved, a long-term legacy resides for individuals, teams and organisations. Critically reflecting on where the energy needs to be focused for relationships to support learning involves taking a systems view. This can help you understand which relationships might be most important to foster to enhance social workers' learning.

It is common in leadership and organisational development to explore personal networks and circles of influence (Covey, 1992). While there are many issues that we may be concerned about, there are only some people and things that we can influence. While Covey argues that there is little point trying to change things out of your circle of influence, the role of social work is often to try to do so particularly in the interests of furthering social justice. The first step is to consider who is in, and who should be in, your learning network. How important your different relationships are in relation to your learning can then be mapped. The final steps are to reflect on how effective the different relationships are and whether any need improvement. A stakeholder mapping of this type can provide insight into the network of relationships, the broader ecosystem and prompt awareness into where things can be strengthened.

Relationships are fundamental to leadership and positive influence. Yukl (2013) suggests positive tactics that include inspirational appeal, consultation, collaboration and exploring how your request is of benefit to another person. Negative tactics, however, are commonly seen where unreasonable requests, pressure and personal appeals (Yukl, 2013) can have a disastrous effect on the development of effective relationships for learning. Simpson et al. (2017) found that theories of conflict resolution were needed to understand the environment for continuing professional development in integrated services. Knowledge and skills from practice in health and social care are readily transferable to learning relationships. Bridges and Fuller (2015) highlight the importance of the relational capacity of practitioners as fundamental in a compassionate learning and caring environment.

Core social work skills and knowledge that support the development of effective learning relationships include listening, communicating, planning and understanding the context of people's lives.

Learning in practice

I learnt a lot from other people, people that I respect and I think that is probably where the best of my learning has come from, seeing practice that I'd want to copy and seeing practice that I wouldn't want to copy, to shape me to be kind of who I wanted to be but also seeing how clients, to use that word, how they respond to different people.

(Chloe in Ferguson, 2021, p92)

Reflective questions

- What relationships matter to you in your role?
- How has your learning been influenced by relationships with other people?
- Who do you want to develop stronger relationships with to promote learning?

Summary points

- Scotland has great opportunities to strengthen networks and relationships for professional learning.
- Learning from lived experiences is essential for social workers.
- Learning with other social workers is essential throughout the career.
- Keep focused on why relationships matter to professional practice with people.

Further reading

A quick read

Anne Duddington, David Gowar and Kay Wall's article 'Nothing about us without us: The voices of people with lived experience in practice education and post-qualifying social work' is recommended by Daniel.

Helpful resources

The dedicated NQSW website holds carefully curated resources on peer learning, learning through supervision and guidance for employers about supporting learning. Other resources recommended by Scottish social workers are highlighted in the final section of this book, many of which relate to learning with others.

A deeper dive

The final report on the longitudinal study into NQSW experiences in Scotland by Trish McCulloch, Scott Grant and other colleagues is great to contextualise the importance of relationships for learning that set the foundations in the early career.

Please also see the resources section in the Appendix.

Many thanks to Daniel Piggins for getting into conversation with me and sharing his experience.

References

Bell, J, Fraser, M, Hitchin, S, McCulloch, L and Morrison, L (2020) 'Planning and delivering a skills practice workshop', in McLaughlin, H, Duffy, J, Beresford, P, Casey, H and Cameron, C (eds) *The Routledge handbook of service user involvement in human services research and education*, Routledge, London, pp. 239–349.

Bolger, J (2019) 'Inter-professional education/learning across social work education provision in Scotland', *Journal of Further and Higher Education*, 44(5): 705–715, https://doi.org/10.1080/0309877x.2019.1576861.

Bridges, J and Fuller, A (2015) 'Creating learning environments for compassionate care: A programme to promote compassionate care by health and social care teams', *International Journal of Older People Nursing*, 10(1): 48–58, https://doi.org/10.1111/opn.12055.

Cabiati, E and Levy, S (2021) 'Inspiring conversations: A comparative analysis of the involvement of experts by experience in Italian and Scottish social work education', *The British Journal of Social Work*, 51(2): 487–504, https://doi.org/10.1093/bjsw/bcaa163.

Covey, S (1992) *Principle-centred leadership*, Simon & Schuster, London.

Dictionaries of the Scots Language [online] https://www.dsl.ac.uk/entry/snd/munsie/.

Duddington, A, Gowar, D and Wall, K (April 2023) 'Nothing about us without us: The voices of people with lived experience in practice education and post-qualifying social work', The *British Journal of Social Work*, 53(3): 1766–1774, https://doi.org/10.1093/bjsw/bcad086.

Duffy, J and Beresford, P (2020) 'Critical issues in the development of service user involvement', Chapter 1 in McLaughlin, H, Beresford, P, Cameron, C, Casey, H and Duffy, J (eds) *The Routledge handbook of service user involvement in human services research and education*, Routledge, London, pp. 9–17.

Eno, S and Kerr, J (2013) 'That was awful! I'm not ready yet, am I?' Is there such a thing as a Good Fail?', *Journal of Practice Teaching and Learning*, 11(3): 135–148, https://doi.org/10.1921/jpts.v11i3.274.

Ferguson, G (2021) '"When David Bowie created Ziggy Stardust" the lived experiences of social workers learning through work', Doctor of Education (EdD) Thesis, The Open University.

Ferguson, G (2022) *The importance of workplace learning for social workers* [online] www.iriss.org.uk/sites/default/files/2022-12/insights-67.pdf.

Finch, J (2017) *Supporting struggling students on placement: A practical guide*, Policy Press, Bristol.

Gee, M, Ager, W and Haddow, A (2009) 'The caring experience: Learning about community care through spending 24 hours with people who use services and family carers', *Social Work Education*, 28(7): 691–706, https://doi.org/10.1080/02615470802404200.

Giesler, MA (2021) 'Humanizing oppression: The value of the human library experience in social work education', *Journal of Social Work Education*, 58(2): 390–402, https://doi.org/10.1080/10437797.2021.1885541.

Grant, S, McCulloch, T, Daly, M and Kettle, M (2022) *Newly qualified social workers in Scotland: A five-year longitudinal study final report* [online] https://www.sssc.uk.com/publications/downloads/2025/04/Newly-qualified-social-workers-in-Scotland-a-five-year-longitudinal-study.pdf.

Ingram, R and Smith, M (2018) *Relationship-based practice: Emergent themes in social work literature* [online] https://www.iriss.org.uk/resources/insights/relationship-based-practice-emergent-themes-social-work-literature.

Levy, S, Cabiati, E, Dow, J, Dowson, E, Swankie, K and Martin, G (2021) 'Reflections on inspiring conversations in social work education: The voices of Scottish experts by experience and Italian students', in Driessens, K and Lyssens-Danneboom, V (eds) *Service users in social work education, research and policy: A comparative European analysis*, Policy Press, Bristol, pp. 97–108.

Moncur, J (2019) *Your other national drink; BARR returns to 100-year-old recipe for new bru*, Daily Record, Glasgow [online] https://link-gale-com.libezproxy.open.ac.uk/apps/doc/A603483337/STND?u=tou&sid=bookmark-STND&xid=9c296eed.

Parker, J (2008) 'When things go wrong! Placement disruption and termination: Power and student perspectives', *British Journal of Social Work*, 40: 983–999, https://doi.org/10.1093/bjsw/bcn149

Ruch, G, Turney, D and Ward, A (2018) *Relationship-based social work: Getting to the heart of practice*, Second edition, Jessica Kingsley, London.

Simpson, JE, Bardsley, J, Haider, S, Bayley, K, Brown, G, Harrington-Vail, A and Dale-Emberton, A (2017) 'Taking advantage of dissonance: A CPD framework', *Journal of Children's Services*, 12(1): 1–15, https://doi.org/10.1108/JCS-11-2016-0020.

SSSC (2019) *Standards in social work education*, Scottish Social Services Council, Dundee [online] https://learn.sssc.uk.com/siswe/siswe.html.

SSSC (2024a) *Core learning elements for social workers: Newly qualified social worker (NQSW) descriptors and mandatory learning activity* [online] https://www.sssc.uk.com/about-us/publications/core-learning-elements-for-social-workers-newly-qualified-social-worker-nqsw-descriptors-and-mandatory-learning-activity/.

SSSC (2024b) *Peer supervision and mentoring* [online] https://www.nqsw.sssc.uk.com/resource/peer-supervision-and-mentoring/.

Vallely, J (2020) *Navigating evidence* [online] https://www.iriss.org.uk/resources/tools/navigating-evidence.

Wareing, M and Ferguson, G (2024) 'Learning environments', in Wareing, M (ed) *Practice supervision and assessment in nursing, health and social care*, Routledge, Abingdon, pp. 27–39.

Yukl, GA (2013) *Leadership in organizations*, Eighth edition, Prentice-Hall, Upper Saddle River.

Chapter 10

Supervising, facilitating and assessing social work practice learning

Introduction

This final chapter speaks mainly to those in a direct practice educator role (although it is equally valuable for learners and others involved in supporting them) and turns to the individual relationships in which learning is supervised and assessed. It links to all the other ideas included throughout the book so far. Approaches to effective supervision and support for individual learners are explored. Assessing learning against criteria and standards in qualifying programmes or specialist awards in Scotland is also discussed. Fundamental principles of fair and robust assessment which model social work values and skills are considered. Managing complex issues such as fitness to practice, ethical dilemmas and students who have not met assessment criteria is explored in the context of the relationships that need to support these processes across organisations and educational providers. Social work educators need to use theories of learning and social work in approaching their role drawing together this expertise to support, facilitate and assess learners in their practice.

Chapter aims

By the end of this chapter, you will be able to:

- identify the theories which inform a practice educator role;
- describe the principles of fair assessment;
- consider how to develop an ethical pathway for assessing learning.

Facilitating learning

To effectively facilitate learning in a Scottish social work context all that has come in the previous chapters provides the foundation for the practice educator role. In summary, it is vital to understand the history and context for practice learning, the importance of learning in direct practice, leadership for learning, preparation for learning, learning as a social work student in Scotland, learning in diverse practice settings and creating effective environments and relationships for learning. All these areas form the curriculum in Scottish practice education courses. Social work educators need to use educational as well as core social work theories in approaching their role, drawing together this expertise to support, facilitate and assess learners in their practice. There is therefore a twin-track of

DOI: 10.4324/9781041057598-14

research and theoretical evidence that needs to inform what educators do. This book is heavily influenced by evidence from Scottish empirical research into how social workers learn in their practice and sector knowledge from the practice learning community.

Understanding learners and learning

Lots of ideas about learning and individual learners have featured in earlier chapters. It is important to keep thinking about what we mean by learning and learning needs, preferences or styles (including our own) in planning to support learners. The resources which are signposted throughout the book also provide a greater grounding in theories about learning for those who are studying to be a practice educator or who are interested in this. Learning is sometimes described as change or growth in knowledge or skills. Carl Rogers's theories that are most usually associated with therapeutic work are highly influential to understanding learning and personal growth. The core conditions of helping relationships such as empathy, congruence and unconditional positive regard (Rogers, 1980) stem from Rogers's work as an educationalist, highlighting these as essential for enabling learning. There is therefore a clear parallel between what is helpful for practice relationships and those which foster learning. Understanding the individual learner and your self-awareness as an educator is essential as part of your own reflexive process. It is commonly reported that people's teaching practices are likely to be shaped by their own experiences. Thinking about power specifically is also important in any learning context.

Reflective questions

- What are the power dynamics in practice education generally?
- What are some specific issues of potential power imbalance in any individual learner/ practice educator relationship?
- How can you bring these power dynamics into your discussion as a practice educator?

Learning, transformation and liberation

Learning is fundamentally transformative (Mezirow, 1990), inextricably linked with empowerment and liberation (Freire, 1970) at individual and societal levels. In *Teaching to Transgress*, learning *is* freedom (Hooks, 1994) recognising the political and anti-oppressive nature of education fundamental to social justice. Social work educators therefore ought to be well placed to grapple with the power dynamics of learning relationships. Some favourite theories that are likely to inform the vision and practice of educators in social work (with just some examples of influential theorists in parentheses) include:

- principles of adult learning (Malcolm Knowles, Peter Jarvis, Mark Tennant);
- workplace learning (Knud Illeris, Joseph Raeline, Carol Costley);
- professional learning (Michael Eraut);
- learning organisations, cultures and communities (Peter Senge, Jean Lave, Etienne and Beverley Wenger, Yves Engström, Edgar Schein);
- reflective learning (David Kolb, Donald Schön, Jennifer Moon);
- transformative individual and societal learning (Jack Mezirow, Knud Illeris, Paulo Freire);

- anti-oppressive practice and anti-racist supervision (Prospera Tedam, Jane Dalrymple and Beverley Burke, Shabnam Ahmed).

These examples are just a few of the kinds of theories or thinkers that might inform your approach to understanding and facilitating learning. You will have preferences for what makes sense and is useful to you, in the same way as the students who you are working with. In both cases, it is about applying the theories to dynamic practice situations and keeping an open mind to explore new ideas that are essential for us all. If you are a link worker or practice educator, think about the kinds of theories that you are already aware of and identify what areas of knowledge you need to explore more fully. Understanding different models of supervision is also essential for the link worker and practice educator role.

It would be remiss of this book not to explicitly mention the importance of decolonising social work education, theory and practice. Dula (2024) provides a helpful chapter on postcolonial theories for social workers to overcome a Western view of social work, one of many resources available from the International Federation of Social Workers. In a manifesto of what decolonial education can be, Dennis (2025) suggests we need to put theorists in their place, acknowledging their time and context. It is a challenge to consider the position of widely used theories and the place of theorists when some have been (and continue to be) silenced and erased (Dennis, 2025). In practice education, all that we do should model anti-oppressive practices.

Learning in practice

My first practice educator suggested that I complete my practice educator course as soon as I could, as being able to explain theory and practice to others would prompt me to keep learning and developing. She was absolutely right as it made me read more widely and engage in developing policy. It helped to look at the wider picture beyond the narrow focus of the work I was involved in and allowed me to make connections between national government work and what that meant for the people we worked with.

(Practice educator Scotland)

Supervising learning

It is beyond the scope of this book to cover the knowledge and skills of professional supervision; many excellent resources cover this theory and practice (e.g., Kettle, 2015; SSSC, 2016, 2024). Kettle (2015) provides an excellent overview and critical appraisal of supervision in the context of Scottish practice which includes discussion on the 4 × 4 × 4 model of supervision Wonnacott (2012) developed from the work of Toni Morrison.

Many social work and learning and development teams will have used Morrison's texts for many years to inform supervision in social work. If you see copies of these spiral bound masterpieces lurking on someone's bookshelf, use them and treasure them. Of course, there are many supervision models and approaches, but the 4 × 4 × 4 model is

Table 10.1 Elements of supervision for learning

Functions of supervision

Managerial
Competent, accountable performance is connected to how social workers learn to
  undertake social work tasks in the practice context.
Formative
Continuing professional development is clearly explicit in connection to learning and a key
  focus of the supervision approach
Supportive
Personal support involves the whole of the person in the process, the deeply personal
  journey of learning as a social worker.
Mediation
Engaging the individual with the organisation connects the individual process with the
  landscape and places of practice, organisational learning cultures and the ecosystem of
  professional learning.

Stakeholders in supervision

Service users
People using services are at the heart of practice and therefore essential to be at the centre
  of learning through supervision
Workers
Supervision should be a protected and safe reflective space for social workers to learn from
  their own practice and shared experiences
Organisation
Supervision is a leadership space in which organisations can support ethical conditions for
  learning and social workers' support.
Partners
Understanding the different perspectives of partners and other stakeholders is fundamental
  to critical reflection.

Stages in supervision

Experience (what happened?) – *Reflection* (what was it like?) – *Analysis* (what does this
  mean?) – *Action Plan* (what next?)
The supervision process embeds the cycle of experiential and reflective learning (Kolb,
  1984) using skills to promote awareness, understanding and meaning for moving forward
  in practice.

helpful to consider here as we begin to focus on learning through supervision. Engagement as a student sets the foundation for professional supervision thereafter. In simple
terms, the model draws together four functions, four stakeholders and four stages of supervision. Table 10.1 summarises how learning is connected to all of the elements not only
the formative function of supervision.

While Table 10.1 provides a rudimentary outline of supervision elements, the role that
supervision plays is very clear. The supervisory process is one undertaken by link workers,
practice educators and line managers at different stages, but there are common aspects.

Reflective questions

- What are the things you are trying to encourage in supervision for learning?
- What are the tools or frameworks that you can use to guide you?
- How might supervision of students differ from later stages?

You might have reflected on your own experiences of supervision, which is important to do as this will influence what you consider an important focus or style. You might use tools to support reflection (SSSC, 2019) or the anti-racist supervision template (Ahmed, 2022) to support supervision. If you are a learner, you might have reflected on how it feels and the power dynamics of the supervision relationship. One of the major differences in supervision for social work students or those undertaking a post-qualifying award such as the practice educator qualification is that learning is being assessed.

Assessing learners

Linked with the role of the practice educator is the importance of fair and ethical assessment. This is also relevant for those who are assessing people undertaking their practice educator qualification or for those who are assessing social workers undertaking specialist qualifications such as the Mental Health Officer (MHO) award. The assessment process is significant for the learner, determining their progression towards achieving their qualification. It is central to their experience as a learner, and the practice educator has a key role in modelling ethical assessment for future practice. The experience of assessment within practice learning, usually through the vehicle of the supervision relationship, provides the learner with a model for professional practice and service user relationships. The term 'assessment' can have different meanings, so it is important to be clear about what this involves in social work practice learning. Assess is a form of the Latin verb *assidere*, to 'sit with'. It is something therefore that we do with and for the learner, not something we do to them. An assessment is a comprehensive multifaceted analysis of performance; it must be based on evidence drawn from authentic practice tasks.

Reflective questions

- What are the standards that you would be assessing a student/learner against?
- Where would you gather evidence from?
- How would you ensure that assessment was fair and robust?

It is essential for any learner to understand what they are being assessed on and how evidence is gathered (see Chapter 4). It is also highly likely that providing feedback at different stages would be a central element of your approach in facilitating learning and adapting assessment tasks to fit learner needs. You might also have reflected on your previous experience as a practice educator and how the assessment process felt.

Assessing against standards and frameworks

Assessment of social work students, practice educators, MHOs and students in vocational qualifications in Scotland is clearly informed by set criteria for evidence that needs to be generated and reviewed by an assessor as to whether it is sufficient. You are making a judgement as a practice educator, but the assessment judgement needs to be related to the requirements you are assessing the learner on. It is essential therefore to understand these and to have discussed these with the learner.

This chapter will not dwell on situations where students do not meet the standards, that is, will have a fail recommendation for their practice learning, but this is undoubtedly and understandably very difficult for anyone involved. There is excellent research and resources from Finch (2017) and Finch and Tedam (2023) on issues relating to learners who are not progressing to meet the requirements in practice learning and from Eno and Kerr (2013) on how sometimes a failed placement can be perceived positively. Often practice educators are concerned about when students or apprentices are not progressing well, but having a clear plan and pathway through the stages of your role can help support a fair assessment process. The role of a practice educator is fundamentally the same irrespective of the outcome: to create supportive conditions for learning; be clear about how learning will be assessed; provide feedback on evidence; make a professional judgement on whether evidence is sufficient to meet the criteria and communicate the assessment decision clearly and timeously. The student needs to be an active participant in the whole of the process.

Ethical assessment

Ethical assessment is always about being clear and framing feedback in relation to the standards you are assessing against. Setting out the ways in which you will gather evidence and provide feedback should be clearly negotiated in a practice learning agreement and woven through your practice education. Linda Grierson has been at the helm of practice learning in Scotland in many roles supporting social workers' learning, including as former chair of the Scottish Organisation for Practice Teaching (ScOPT). Linda developed and promoted a comprehensive ethical assessment pathway for practice learning in her teaching of practice educators and link workers (Grierson, 2024). This pathway is depicted visually with interconnected stages leading from the pre-placement phase through to an evidence-based recommendation. All the stages of the placement, from before it begins and right through to the end, are important for creating the supervisory alliance and reviewing progress. The pathway rests on a partnership approach with shared responsibility for learning between the student, practice educator and link worker.

Ideally, this ethical assessment approach seeks to acknowledge and equalise the power between partners in the assessment process. The Practice Educator is acknowledged as having the power to recommend a pass or fail, but the student has the power to show that they have passed through the evidence that they demonstrate (Grierson, 2024). At different stages, it is essential to be clear about expectations, and if the foundation is not negotiated well, then problems will arise.

Stages in practice learning and assessment

Practice educators often think about placements in key stages in which there are both formative and summative assessment points. If you are involved in assessing a social worker (or being assessed) on a different programme such as the practice educator course, there are similar principles. Practice educator programmes and university practice learning guidance will also relate to roles, tasks, timelines and expectations. These are usually detailed and share similar principles although there may be some differences in templates for evidence and reporting used. There are plenty books and resources available on the practicalities of practice learning but take care as some are mapped to standards which are not relevant in Scotland (such as England's Professional Capabilities Framework (PCF) and Practice Educator Professional Standards (PEPS)).

First half of the placement

The pre-placement stage is characterised by preparation and planning and informed by knowledge of what will be required. The practice educator or link worker will prepare the team, arrange induction tasks and consider the level of student. The student will plan practical arrangements and familiarise themselves with the Standards in Social Work Education (SiSWE) and Codes of Practice along with other expectations. Reasonable adjustments also need to be discussed (see Chapter 4).

At the beginning stage, once placement starts, there needs to be clear induction. This is so important that the University of Stirling Practice Educator programme foregrounds the requirement for a robust induction plan as part of their assessment of practice educators. Negotiation of workload, requirements of placement and beginning to track evidence against the SiSWE need to be woven through all stages. The SiSWE are not separate to practice; they describe the skills, knowledge and competence of social work, and are helpful in articulating the microdetails.

Consider where the evidence will come from. Typically, evidence is generated from verbal and written reflection or tasks, work products, direct observation, feedback from people using the service, colleagues and the link worker. A record or tracker, a simple table of the SiSWE with notes on what evidence is generated from an early stage can help for consolidation and confidence. Notes from supervision of learning remain an important aspect of practice learning which are important for tracking progress but also in modelling professional record-keeping principles.

At the interim stage, towards the middle of the placement, it is essential that everyone is clear on progress and that an assessment decision is communicated clearly. There is usually a formal university process or meeting to record the details of this. Priority actions for the remainder of the placement need to be agreed and thereafter monitored. A helpful technique is to ask the student to rate their progress against the SiSWE, identifying how they are doing, why the evidence supports this and what they consider as the next steps. The practice educator can then share their perspective.

Second half of the placement

The student will continue to develop and deepen their knowledge and skills, consolidating learning and focusing on the priority areas identified. Practice demonstrated well in the first half needs to be maintained and enhanced where necessary. Checking in clearly on progress against the SiSWE as the placement moves towards the ending stage is essential to allow time to address feedback and maximise opportunities to evidence what is required. Students need to understand what will be required for them to have met the SiSWE; this can't be left vague. Within all of these stages, there needs to be a clear negotiation of what is required, who needs to do it and integration of the perspectives on how things are going. There should be progressive development of learning through the use of feedback to inform this. Grierson's pathway highlights the responsibility of the student to show initiative and responsibility for learning and assessment throughout the process.

As the placement moves towards the end stages, practice educators have to make their evidence-informed recommendation as to whether the standards are met or otherwise. As with any other social work assessment, judgement or decision – this needs to be articulated clearly, based on critical appraisal and synthesis of the evidence. Practice educator reports also need to be professional and articulated in relation to the SiSWE and based on evidence in the same way as other social work reports.

There needs to be a continuous feedback and refinement cycle with students demonstrating their being active in the process. A former colleague of mine used to question 'who is doing all the work?' when I was first a practice educator; the rhetorical question is always a moment of pause and recalibration. Grierson highlights that students need to evaluate their own performance in the process. A checklist of things to remember at each stage is also often used by practice educators to inform each stage.

Many helpful examples of structured ways to support learning were included in the ScOPT Toolkit which was available through ScOPT. If you don't have this, ask around as someone close to you will probably have a copy. At the time of writing. this is not available online, but you can easily create your own range of tools. This chapter has scratched the surface of issues relating to supervising, facilitating and assessing learning. Collective wisdom across practice educators in Scotland is a rich source of support and part of the professional learning ecosystem. There will be local opportunities for you to connect with other practice educators in your own organisation, at events held by different universities and through national initiatives. You are an important part of this community and the professional learning ecosystem whatever your role.

Learning in practice

The commitment of workers to continue providing services when stretched ignites my drive to support the development of robust, supported and confident social workers. It inspired me to undertake my PLQ in practice educating so I could learn best how to use my practice knowledge and experience to facilitate and support practice placements for students, enabling access to more statutory placements. The learning culture within my authority is hugely supportive. I'm given time and support with any identified professional development which is crucial.

(Practice educator Scotland)

Reflective questions

- How will you plan for effective and ethical assessment of learners?
- Who are the people who can support you in your role?
- What resources do you already have and where will you explore for others?

Summary of key points

- Practice educators and link workers are central to facilitating and assessing learning.
- An ethical approach to assessment is needed to form a well-evidenced recommendation.
- Students need to be active in the process of their learning and assessment.
- The practice educator community is a central source of expertise and resources.

Further reading

A quick read

Martin Kettle's *Achieving Effective Supervision* published as an Iriss Insight in 2015 is a fantastic, comprehensive overview of the evidence for supervision, key research and theory (https://www.iriss.org.uk/resources/insights/achieving-effective-supervision).

A helpful set of resources

The dedicated SiSWE website has great resources to support critical reflection and plan for placements (https://learn.sssc.uk.com/siswe). Sets of supervision resources for social workers and for supervisors are a fantastic inclusion in the suite of materials available as part of the NQSW Supported Year in Scotland; they are evidence-based and connected to the key theories of supervision and peer learning which you can explore further (https://www.nqsw.sssc.uk.com/resource/supervision-resources-for-nqsws/).

A deeper dive

Contemporary Theories of Learning: Learning Theorists … In Their Own Words edited by Knud Illeris is a fantastic compendium of pieces about key theories written by world-renowned experts.

Please also see the resources section in the Appendix.

Many thanks to Linda Grierson for getting into conversation with me and sharing her wisdom.

References

Ahmed, S (2022) 'Anti-racist supervision template', in Reid, W and Ahmed, S (eds) *Anti-racist supervision benefits all* [online] https://basw.co.uk/sites/default/files/2024-06/BPS%20%26%20 SOS%20article%20-%20Anti-racist%20supervision%20benefits%20all_0.pdf.

Dennis, A (2025) *Decolonial dreams: The unmarked scholar reimagines the purpose of post-16 education* inaugural lecture [online] https://research.open.ac.uk/events/decolonial-dreams-unmarked-scholar-reimagines-purpose-post-16-education.

Dula, E (2024) 'Global entanglements: Introduction to postcolonial theories and their relevance for social work', in Dula, E, Dhananka, S and Truell, R (eds) *Social work as a global profession* [online] https://www.ifsw.org/product/books/social-work-as-a-global-profession-handbook-for-teaching-and-learning/.

Eno, S and Kerr, J (2013) ''That was awful! I'm not ready yet, am I?' Is there such a thing as a Good Fail?', *Journal of Practice Teaching and Learning*, 11(3): 135–148.

Finch, J (2017) *Supporting struggling students on placement: A practical guide*, Policy Press, Bristol.

Finch, J and Tedam, P (2023) 'Failure to fail or fast tracking to failure: A critical exploration of social work placements', *Social Work Education*, 43(7): 2024–2039.

Freire, P (1970) *Pedagogy of the oppressed*, Seabury Press, New York.

Grierson, L (2024) *Ethical assessment pathway for link workers and practice educators*, Perth and Kinross Council, Perth.

Hooks, B (1994) *Teaching to transgress: Education as the practice of freedom*, Routledge, New York.

Kettle, M (2015) *Achieving effective supervision* [online] https://www.iriss.org.uk/resources/insights/achieving-effective-supervision.

Kolb, DA (1984) *Experiential learning: Experience as the source of learning and development*, Prentice Hall, Englewood Cliffs.

Mezirow, J (1990) *Fostering critical reflection in adulthood: A guide to transformative and emancipatory learning*, Jossey-Bass, San Francisco.

Rogers, C (1980) *A way of being*, Houghton Mifflin, New York.

SSSC (2016) *Supervision learning resource* [online] https://stepintoleadership.info/assets/pdf/SSSC-Supervision-learning-resource-Sept-16.pdf.

SSSC (2019) *Standards in social work education*, Scottish Social Services Council, Dundee [online] https://learn.sssc.uk.com/siswe/siswe.html.

SSSC (2024) *Supervision resources for supervisors* [online] https://www.nqsw.sssc.uk.com/resource/supervision-resources-for-managers-and-supervisors.

Wonnacott, J (2012) *Mastering social work supervision*, Jessica Kingsley, London.

Conclusion

The book has discussed the Scottish context of social workers' learning and has stressed the importance of how practice fosters development throughout the career. Reflection is embedded in the profession and collectively doing so to learn from shared wisdom and experience is essential for a flourishing professional learning ecosystem. Scotland has a great opportunity to strengthen how such a system becomes more cohesive. Things are changing at the time of writing in terms of the structures that oversee the profession in Scotland. The book has focused on what matters in social workers' professional learning, the nature and practice context of that learning which will endure irrespective of how structures organise. That everyone is a learner, everyone is an educator and everyone is a leader was proposed in the early sections of the book. Opportunities to strengthen how learning is supported rely on understanding and using the kinds of theories that we use in the profession about relationships, learning organisations, cultures, systems thinking and design principles. In summary, the book tries to promote a simple idea, that strengthening professional learning simultaneously strengthens the social work profession. Conceptualising learning this way enables social work to continue to develop a way to articulate its unique contribution to Scotland. Understanding the complexity of learning for social workers goes some way towards explaining just what this extraordinary job involves.

Slàinte Mhath, best wishes on your social work travels in this extraordinary job.

DOI: 10.4324/9781041057598-15

A guide to learning resources around Scotland

Welcome to this guide which takes us on a trip around Scotland with messages from social workers about people, places, spaces and resources that have supported or inspired their learning. A survey in 2025 asked social workers, managers and educators what had inspired their learning. Ideas generated from this survey have informed this guide.

Postcards from learning

To: Social workers and practice educators, Scotland

Hi, what has inspired me is probably my practice placement as a student in a children and families team and that all I learned from wonderful colleagues. My social work degree was excellent. I studied to become a practice educator, it's so important to explore and develop so that I can support student social workers. I also learned so much knowledge and research on a Child Protection Post Graduate qualification too. I have always been inspired by SASW and BASW who deliver excellent webinars and offer support to social workers in terms of professional development. I thoroughly enjoy IRISS insights and have peer reviewed some of these as it relates to my practice setting. This has been excellent to be at the beating heart of policy and research in practice. Being together in reflective spaces is brilliant but doesn't happen often enough. I think it's about being inspired and finding out who inspires you and tapping into that knowledge. However, it's about giving back to the profession and inspiring others in practice too!

Social Work Manager, Glasgow

What people have inspired social workers' learning around Scotland?

Here are just some of the ways in which people have inspired learning. How does this fit with your experience as a learner or educator? These contributions really echo the messages from Chapter 9 about learning relationships.

Individual people that show a love and passion for learning and the profession. No hierarchies in learning environments.

(Learning and Development Lead, Tayside)

Being part of a foster family has inspired me to become a social worker. Working closely with my little brother's social workers over the years and seeing the impact they can have on someone. Being able to relate to the struggles and frustrations from a family point of view allows me to adapt the work I carry out to benefit the family/person.

(SW Student Tayside)

My learning has been inspired by hands on experience and receiving feedback from others. I have also been inspired by shadowing colleagues.

(SW Student Edinburgh)

Our learning and development team are proactive, supportive and organised! They have facilitated lots of learning opportunities for the social work service, inspired collaborative working with other professionals and colleagues.

(Social worker Tayside)

Mentorship from academics, lecturers and fellow social workers. SASW monthly student / NQSW meeting. This gave courage to try new ideas, supported me when things didn't go to plan, gave me room to discuss thinking.

(NQSW Renfrewshire)

The families I work with inspire me every day. My job is full of learning and understanding why people behave in certain ways which I love. I have learned about things such as addiction that I have never experienced but I build relationships where families are able to share with me what it is like for them. This alongside further reading helps me understand and do my job better.

(Social worker West Lothian)

What places and spaces have inspired social workers' learning around Scotland?

All the places where social workers are undertaking their placements, working and the organisations that support the profession have inspired learning. What do you think? What counts as a place for learning? Here are just some of the places around Scotland that support and inspire social workers' learning. Would you identify different ones?

Being able to access different organisations, hear range of speakers through events and webinars as well as opportunity to meet with multi-agency partners and practitioners has all contributed to my learning.

(Social worker Central)

I particularly enjoy in person training sessions. I find these are more likely to encourage good conversations and learning compared to individual reading or online group training. I enjoy legislation and policy-based training when new acts or policies are brought out as it is easy to identify exactly how this will be used in our day-to-day work.

(Social worker Angus)

Learning for me was, and is, about opportunities for experiential learning within and across professions and sharing the stories and experiences of the people we serve.

(Social work educator Scotland)

Work in a team where your personal interests are supported and encouraged to grow. Recognition that all having different interests and expertise means a more well-rounded team with lots to share.

(Social Worker Falkirk)

I started my career in residential childcare and this inspired me to go to university to obtain my social work degree. I feel social work could be more promoted in colleges as a career choice in subjects like childcare as this was my path. College was a very positive experience for me as it allowed me to realise university was achievable.

(Social worker West Lothian)

Postcards from learning

To: Social workers and practice educators, Scotland

Hi, The creativity and imagination of the third sector has been a massive influence on my learning as a social worker. It is here that I have found the scope to engage with the rich experiences of individuals, families and communities, who either make use of social work/broader support services or who don't, because what is on offer doesn't work for them. In terms of my learning, I realised that although we often talk about being need-led, we don't always take the time to listen to the stories people tell us and so often we don't really understand the issues or needs. Being in a space where this was possible, and where creative solutions can be explored alongside those seeking help, has challenged the way I think about and understand lots of different issues. Most of all, it has rooted my learning in the connections and relationships we make with those around us. I hope I model this in my role as a practice educator, where I encourage learners to 'take a walk in their client's shoes' the expert. In considering service users as holding the expertise in their own lives and experiences, I have been able to reflect on how I approach my roles as a leader within my organisation; a leader for learning; and leadership in terms of membership of my profession.

Third Sector CEO, Tayside

Scotland-wide places and organisations

Some examples of organisations which have been highlighted by students, social workers and practice educators are included here. It is essential to remember that there are many other specialist services relating to specific areas of practice that have up-to-date research and practice resources. Many local areas host superb communities of practice and peer learning opportunities such as Perth and Kinross (https://www.pklearning.org.uk/Community-of-Practice).

Iriss

https://www.iriss.org.uk/
Iriss remains the go-to place for social workers for up-to-date research and evidence summaries. Iriss aims to help the social work and social care sector flourish through research, improvement and innovation. Research insights are superb, but there are also incredible learning materials such as *Writing Analysis in Social Care*, *Gypsy/Traveller Intersectionality: Strengthening the Role of Social Work* and Adult and Child Protection-focused resources. Go forth and explore!

Social Work Scotland

https://socialworkscotland.org/
Social Work Scotland is the professional body for social work leaders in Scotland. As a member-led organisation, they represent the profession at a local and national level, influencing policy and legislation, and advocating for a sustainable workforce. Rooted in social work values, they support and develop leaders in the profession to champion social justice, navigate challenging contexts and help shape the future of social work in Scotland. A fantastic range of publications, reports and guidance are available along with the details of current projects and standing committees. Keep updated!

Scottish Social Services Council

https://www.sssc.uk.com
The Scottish Social Services Council (SSSC) has been at the fore of providing learning resources since its inception, developing creative learning resources and guidance for all stages of social workers' learning. These are just some highlights of the resources available.

- Standards in Social Work Education (https://learn.sssc.uk.com/siswe/siswe.html);
- NQSW Supported Year (https://www.nqsw.sssc.uk.com/nqsw-supported-year/);
- Continuous Professional Learning (https://www.sssc.uk.com/supporting-the-workforce/continuous-professional-learning/);
- Learning Zone (https://www.sssc.uk.com/supporting-the-workforce/learning-zone/).

SSSC MyLearning service is a suite of digital tools and services which has been designed to support learners with their continuous professional learning journey (https://learn.sssc.uk.com/mylearning/).

Highly recommended curated resources on policy, legislation and practice guidance across Scottish practice settings developed to support social workers to return to practice during COVID-19 pandemic are relevant for anyone to access. This is a superb collection in one place that supports the understanding of Scottish social work along with the range of places to get the information you need to learn (https://learn.sssc.uk.com/bitesizeguides/socialwork).

Other fantastic resources developed and hosted in the Step into Leadership website are the following: *Coaching Learning Resource, Mentoring Guidance, Supervision Learning Resource* and the *Facilitating Learning Resource Pack*, which can be found at this specific link: https://stepintoleadership.info/other_resources.html.

Scottish Association of Social Workers

https://basw.co.uk/about-basw/social-work-around-uk/scottish-association-social-work
The Scottish Association of Social Work (SASW) is the ever-strengthening professional association for social workers in Scotland. The team and national committee work to support members and the social work profession across many agendas. Notable in relation to learning is the Social Work Professional Support Service (SWPSS); regular events and bulletins; specific seminars for NQSWs; and events about the evolving policy landscape. Social workers highlighted SASW for 'campaigning, including policy work challenging government on areas such as domestic abuse, Anti-racism practice and learning from experts by experience. They challenge us all to lobby for change to improve practice for social workers and those using services'. (Social Worker Scotland). Get involved!

NHS Education for Scotland

https://www.nes.scot.nhs.uk/
Along with other materials across workforce development, the Turas eLearning portal developed by National Health Service (NHS) Education for Scotland (NES) is available across the sector and hosts many learning materials of core interest to social workers. Sign up for a Turas account at https://learn.nes.nhs.scot/. This includes resources from the National Trauma Transformation Programme (https://learn.nes.nhs.scot/37896).

The Promise Scotland

https://thepromise.scot/
As well as being the hub for all things The Promise that Scotland made to care experienced children and young people, the website hosts an exceptional suite of learning and development tools based on service design principles. You can also find a specific SSSC resource linking the Codes of Practice to The Promise (https://news.sssc.uk.com/news/helping-you-to-link-the-sssc-codes-uncrc-rights-and-keeping-the-promise).

AFKA Scotland

https://afkascotland.org/
Just one example of an amazing specialist organisation, Association for Fostering, Kinship and Adoption (AFKA) Scotland offers a range of kinship care, fostering and adoption resources to help practitioners develop their practice, learn about the latest research and best practices, and stay informed on legal and regulatory requirements. A superb suite of resources and events are available. AFKA personnel are also at the fore of research and postgraduate study opportunities in this area.

The Children and Young People's Centre for Justice (CYCJ)

https://www.cycj.org.uk/
The CYCJ is another example of a superb specialist organisation that 'constantly produces content on emerging research and learning relating to children in conflict with the law in a range of media (annually updated practice chapter/frequent webinars/monthly e-bulletins)' (Social worker Scotland).

The Scottish Centre for Crime and Justice Research

Another dedicated specialist centre produces research that informs policy and practice and advances understanding of justice. The *Scottish Centre for Crime and Justice Research* (SCCJR) produces research reports, briefing papers, literature reviews, bulletins, written evidence to parliament and more (https://www.sccjr.ac.uk/).

The Mental Welfare Commission for Scotland

https://www.mwcscot.org.uk/
The Mental Welfare Commission for Scotland (MWC) carries out statutory duties to protect and promote the human rights of people with mental illness, learning disabilities, dementia and related conditions but also produces extensive good practice guidance and interactive learning resources. Many resources are available on the Once for Scotland: Adults with Incapacity Learn site on Turas (https://learn.nes.nhs.scot/57826).

The Care Inspectorate

As the regulator for Scottish care services, The Care Inspectorate also develop and host a wide range of good practice learning resources on their main site and specific hub site (https://hub.careinspectorate.com).

Social Work History Network

The Social Work History Network exists to explore the nature and growth of social work in order to inform contemporary policy and practice. An informal network of social workers, historians, archivists, researchers, educators, students and social work policymakers, the Network meets three or four times a year to discuss papers given by invited speakers (https://www.kcl.ac.uk/hscwru/swhn).

The Scottish Government

Direct policy and guidance details from the Scottish Government are essential for reference and keeping up to date with the changing landscape. Some specific areas of relevance are:

- *The National Care Service* (https://www.gov.scot/policies/social-care/national-care-service/);

- *Getting It Right for Every Child* (GIRFEC) (https://www.gov.scot/policies/girfec/girfec-resources/);
- *Looked after Children* (https://www.gov.scot/policies/looked-after-children/);
- *Child Protection* (https://www.gov.scot/policies/child-protection/);
- *Adult Support and Protection* (https://www.gov.scot/policies/social-care/adult-support-and-protection/);
- *Justice Social Work Guidance* (https://www.gov.scot/collections/justice-social-work-guidance/).

Resources

Here are just a few examples of the resources that social workers and practice educators recommend. If you are studying as a social work student or undertaking a practice educator qualification, look to the reading and resources lists which will have been carefully created by the team of experts who have designed the course and are updated regularly. What would you recommend to others? How can you share the things that inspire and support your learning?

> Auditing case files for different purposes - this helped me consider what was best practice/ what others are looking for and how easy it is to miss the child in the adults chaos.
>
> (Social worker Tayside)

> Listening to podcasts specifically helpful social work podcast and Iriss, some examples https://basw.co.uk/training-cpd/lets-talk-social-work-podcast; and previous episodes of IRISS FM podcasts https://directory.libsyn.com/shows/view/id/irissfm.
>
> (NQSW Edinburgh)

> co-working cases with others, creating a learning culture by having team case discussions and being facilitated by a team member.
>
> (Social worker Ayrshire)

> I find research inspiring in offering new insight and bringing a critical lens on practice.
>
> (Social worker Lothians)

> Self-Care Psychology have a great range of resources for supporting practitioner well-being https://www.selfcarepsychology.com/resources.
>
> (Social worker Edinburgh)

> Reflective practice is a cornerstone of Social Work learning and development and again this has been one of the most inspiring ways to learn as a social worker learning from yourself and others. Supervision a much anticipated and enjoyable and interactive learning opportunity. Ring-fenced opportunities to be working alongside experienced colleagues, hearing their conversations, observing their practice and embraced by their humanity and honest fallibility their joy and their commitment to those they work with.
>
> (Social worker Highland)

Made in Scotland

The *Practice Pyramid* developed by Maureen Ross is used by many practice educators and is the subject of a great paper from Jean Gordon and Gillian Mackay on integrating theory and values into practice which is available at https://doi.org/10.1921/jpts.v14i3.1015. The *Theory Circle* from Pat Collingwood is widely used and recommended by students and educators; the full paper describing the model is available at https://doi.org/10.1921/jpts.v6i1.318.

OpenLearn

OpenLearn offers high-quality open access learning resources from the Open University such as *Studying Social Work Law* and *Supporting and Developing Resilience in Social Work* (https://www.open.edu/openlearn). Go explore more!

Siobhan Maclean's resources

Resources created by Siobhan Maclean are a firm favourite of students, social workers and practice educators for their inclusive and interactive content (https://siobhanmaclean.co.uk). Some of the most popular resources (but by no means all) are:

- *Social Care and the Law in Scotland*, 12th edition (Maclean and Shiner) – a really easy-to-digest summary of legislation and a great way to consider what might be relevant to inform practice.
- *Social Work Theory Cards* – easy to use by anyone involved in social work to get into theory and for creative learning activities.
- *Reflective Practice Cards* – a great series of activities and structured focus for critical thinking.
- *Social Work Theory and Practice: A Straightforward Guide*, 4th edition (Maclean and Harrison) – a clear explanation of the major theories used within social work. Ideas about application to practice and suggestions for developing theory informed practice are included throughout.

The Neil Thompson Academy

Neil produces a huge range of materials in support of social work, social care, leadership and many specific topics (https://neilthompson.info).

The Centre for the Advancement of Interprofessional Education

CAIPE works to promote and develop the health and wellbeing of individuals, families and communities through interprofessional education, collaborative practice and related research for workforce development. A vast library of resources is available (https://www.caipe.org/).

Postcards from learning

To: Social workers and practice educators, Scotland

Hi, As a social worker what has inspired my learning has been the desire to do better! I work in children and family services and have a passion to ensure that children are loved, safe and protected. I also enjoy keeping abreast with national practice models, frameworks, policy and legislation and like to research developments to ensure my practice is evidence based and current. I am a trainer in the safe & together model for domestic abuse, the NSPCC reunification framework for return home practice, graded care profile and am really enthused about these. I guess I draw on Siobhan Maclean a lot as I find her resources such as social work theory cards & books, reflective practice cards and videos easy for students to grasp, use, discuss and reflect on. I don't want to be someone who has outdated practice. Working with children in distressing or unsafe situations, child deaths and significant case reviews keep this motivation going for me to continually develop my knowledge, skills and implement these in practice and share that with others.

Social work educator, Tayside

If you took part in the survey, sincere thanks for doing so. It was incredible to hear so many positive examples while acknowledging the context and challenges in which social workers are practising. If you would like more information, fuller reports or resources that are being produced from this research, please contact Dr. Gillian Ferguson at the Open University, gillian.ferguson1@open.ac.uk.

Index

For Product Safety Concerns and Information please contact our EU
representative GPSR@taylorandfrancis.com
Taylor & Francis Verlag GmbH, Kaufingerstraße 24, 80331 München, Germany

www.ingramcontent.com/pod-product-compliance
Lightning Source LLC
Chambersburg PA
CBHW080134270326
41926CB00021B/4478